loaves, cakes &
Quiches

Recipes by Ilona
Photographs by Akiko Ida

HACHETTE
Illustrated

contents

Tips & advice   4

Tomato, basil and mozzarella quiche   6
Pumpkin and cheese quiche   8
Spicy onion quiche   10
Mustard and cheese quiche   12
Spinach and ricotta quiche   14
Munster cheese and bacon quiche   16
Tuna and vegetable quiche   18

Feta cheese and fresh herb loaf   20
Parma ham and fig loaf   22
Roquefort, pear and walnut loaf   24
Mushroom loaf   26
Zucchini and parmesan loaf   28
Green and black olive loaf   30
Bacon, sausage and cheese loaf   32
Salmon, dill and pink peppercorn loaf   34
Sun-dried tomato, caper and basil loaf   36
Pesto and pine nut loaf   38

Strawberry and rhubarb tart	40
Dark chocolate tart	42
Tarte Tatin	44
Raspberry conserve tart	46
Lemon tart	48
Chestnut tart	50
Carrot and walnut cake	52
Lemon poppyseed loaf	54
Candied fruit and nut loaf	56
Apple, raisin and walnut cake	58
Marble cake with almonds	60
Mixed berry loaf	62
Glossary	64

tips & advice

Pesto

Pesto, sometimes called *pistou*, is a thick sauce made from basil, pine nuts, garlic, and olive oil. It is available ready-made in jars, or in the fresh sauce section of large supermarkets. It can also be found at some Italian delicatessens. However, it is easy to make your own.

To make ⅔ cup pesto:
- 3 bunches of fresh basil
- 3 garlic cloves
- ½ cup pine nuts
- 4 tablespoons Parmesan cheese, freshly grated
- 7 tablespoons olive oil
- pinch of coarse salt

Parmesan pie crust

- 2 cups all-purpose flour
- pinch of salt
- 1/4 cup Parmesan cheese, grated
- 4 oz unsalted butter, diced
- 1 egg
- 1 teaspoon sour cream

To make the pastry: Put the flour and salt into a large bowl. Add the butter and with a knife cut it into the flour until evenly distributed, then use your fingertips to rub the fat lightly into the flour until the mixture resembles coarse crumbs. Stir in the cheese. Whisk together the egg and sour cream and add gradually to the crumb mixture (you may not need to use all of it). Using a spatula or a knife, work the mixture together, then use your fingers until you have a smooth dough. Shape into a ball, place in a plastic bag and refrigerate for 1 hour before using.

Sun-dried tomatoes

An authentic Italian *antipasto* ingredient, these are actually made by drying in the sun.
To make your own, cut some tomatoes in half, sprinkle with salt and leave to drain. Arrange the halves on a grill rack set over a baking tin to catch the drips. Put in the oven and bake gently at 300°F for about 3 hours.
Allow to cool completely, then marinate in a lidded glass jar with garlic, olive oil, salt and pepper.
Sun-dried tomatoes can also be bought loose, in packets or in jars from supermarkets and delicatessens.

Poppyseeds

These can be found in the herbs and spices sections of large supermarkets, as well as in health-food shops and delicatessens.

Sweet hazelnut and chocolate pie crust

- 2 cups all-purpose flour
- pinch of salt
- 5½ tablespoons caster sugar
- ⅔ cup ground hazelnuts
- 2 tablespoons unsweetened cocoa powder
- 4 oz unsalted butter
- 1 egg
- 1 teaspoon sour cream

Put the flour and salt into a large bowl. Add the butter and with a knife cut it into the flour until evenly distributed, then use your fingertips to rub the fat lightly into the flour until the mixture resembles coarse crumbs. Stir in the sugar, hazelnuts and cocoa. Whisk together the egg and sour cream and add gradually to the crumb mixture (you may not need all of it). Using a spatula or a knife, work the mixture together, then use your fingers to form a smooth ball of dough. Place in a polythene bag and refrigerate for 1 hour before using.

Bicarbonate of soda

This fine white powder is an indispensable raising agent ingredient when baking sweet cakes. It lightens the mixture and makes it easier to digest. It is readily available in supermarkets and sometimes at the pharmacy (be sure to indicate that it is for culinary use). Always use the quantities indicated in the recipe.

Tomato, basil and mozzarella quiche

For the pie crust
2 cups all-purpose flour
pinch of salt
4 oz unsalted butter, diced
1 egg
1 teaspoon sour cream

For the filling
1 lb tomatoes
4 oz mozzarella
large handful of fresh basil
3 eggs
1 level cup sour cream
salt and pepper

To make the pastry for 1 large tart or 5 small tarts: put the flour and salt into a large bowl. Add the butter and with a knife cut it into the flour until evenly distributed, then use your fingertips to rub the fat lightly into the flour until the mixture resembles coarse crumbs. Whisk together the egg and sour cream and add gradually to the crumb mixture (you may not need to use all of it). Using a spatula or a knife, work the mixture together, then use your fingers until you have a smooth dough. Shape into a ball, put into a plastic bag and refrigerate for 1 hour before using.

Meanwhile, prepare the filling. Place the tomatoes in a bowl and pour over boiling water to cover. Leave for 1–2 minutes, then drain, cut a cross at the stem end of each tomato, and peel off the skins. Seed and chop the flesh. Cut the mozzarella into small cubes. Tear the basil leaves in small pieces by hand or snip with scissors. Whisk together the eggs and sour cream and season with salt and pepper.

Preheat the oven to 375°F. Lightly butter a removable bottom tart pan. Roll out the dough and use to line the pan. Prick the base with a fork.

Arrange the chopped tomato in the crust shell and add the cheese cubes. Sprinkle over the basil leaves and pour over the egg mixture. Bake for 40 minutes. Let cool before unmoulding.

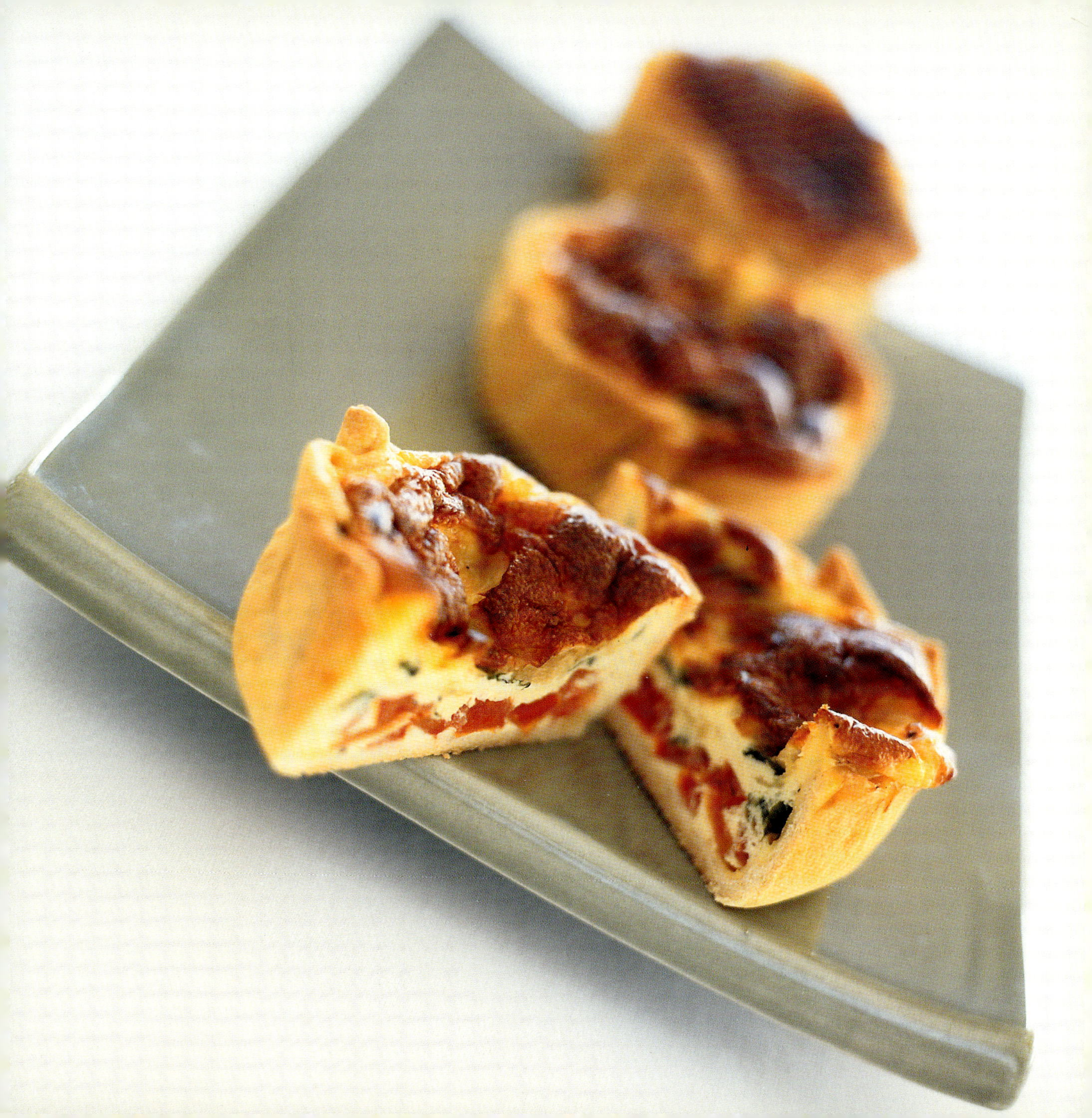

savory quiches

Pumpkin and cheese quiche

For the pie crust
2 cups all-purpose flour
pinch of salt
4 oz unsalted butter, diced
1 egg
1 teaspoon sour cream

For the filling
1 lb pumpkin
2 tablespoons unsalted butter
3 eggs
1 cup grated cheese, such as Gruyère
1 level cup sour cream
handful of fresh cilantro leaves, finely chopped
salt and pepper

To make the pastry: put the flour and salt into a large bowl. Add the butter and with a knife cut it into the flour until evenly distributed, then use your fingertips to rub the fat lightly into the flour until the mixture resembles coarse crumbs. Whisk together the egg and sour cream and add gradually to the crumb mixture (you may not need to use all of it). Using a spatula or a knife, work the mixture together, then use your fingers until you have a smooth dough. Shape into a ball, put into a plastic bag and refrigerate for 1 hour before using.

Preheat the oven to 375°F. Lightly butter a removable bottom tart pan. Roll out the dough and use to line the pan. Prick the base with a fork. Refrigerate until needed.

To make the filling: seed and peel the pumpkin, and cut into small cubes. Melt the butter in a pan, add the pumpkin and cook until tender, about 10 minutes. Add a little water and continue cooking until the pumpkin is tender. Purée and let cool.

In a bowl, whisk together the eggs, cheese, and sour cream. Add the pumpkin purée and mix well. Stir in the cilantro and season to taste with salt and pepper.

Pour into the crust shell and bake for 40 minutes. Let cool slightly before serving.

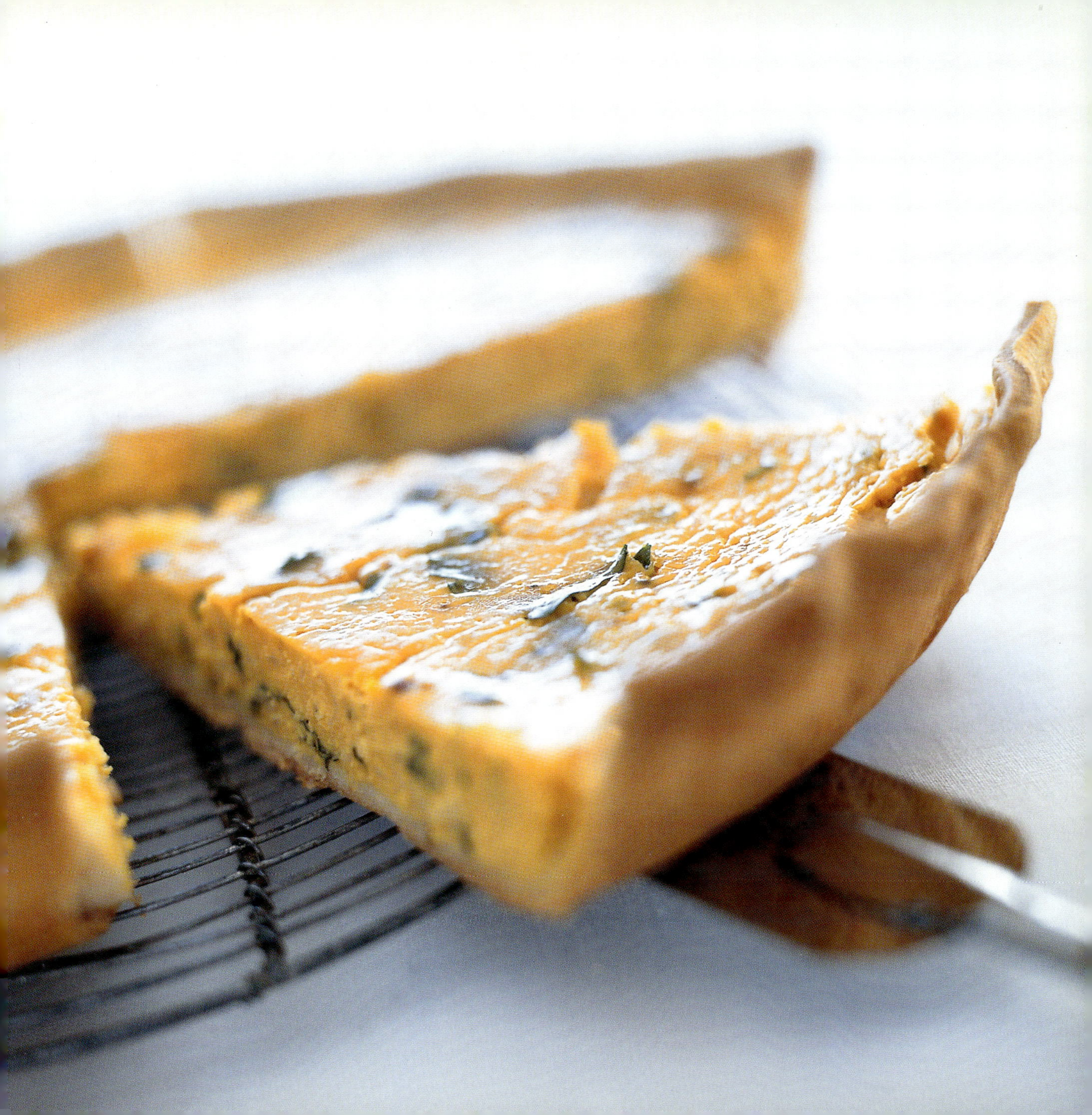

savory quiches

Spicy onion quiche

For the pie crust
2 cups all-purpose flour
pinch of salt
4 oz unsalted butter, diced
1 egg
1 teaspoon sour cream

For the filling
2 oz unsalted butter
2 lb onions, chopped
½ cup dry white wine
1 red chile, seeded and finely chopped
3 eggs
1 level cup sour cream
1 cup finely grated cheese, such as Gruyère
salt and pepper

To make the crust: put the flour and salt into a large bowl. Add the butter and with a knife cut it into the flour until evenly distributed, then use your fingertips to rub the fat lightly into the flour until the mixture resembles coarse crumbs. Whisk together the egg and sour cream and add gradually to the crumb mixture (you may not need to use all of it). Using a spatula or a knife, work the mixture together, then use your fingers until you have a smooth dough. Shape into a ball, put into a plastic bag and refrigerate for 1 hour before using.

Preheat the oven to 375°F. Lightly butter a removable bottom tart pan. Roll out the dough and use to line the pan. Prick all over with a fork. Refrigerate until needed.

To make the filling: melt the butter in a pan, add the onions and cook until soft. Add the wine and chile and simmer gently for 20 minutes. Set aside to cool.

Whisk the eggs in a large bowl. Add the sour cream and the onions and mix well. Season with salt and pepper.

Pour the batter into the crust shell, sprinkle with the cheese and bake for about 45 minutes. Let cool slightly before serving.

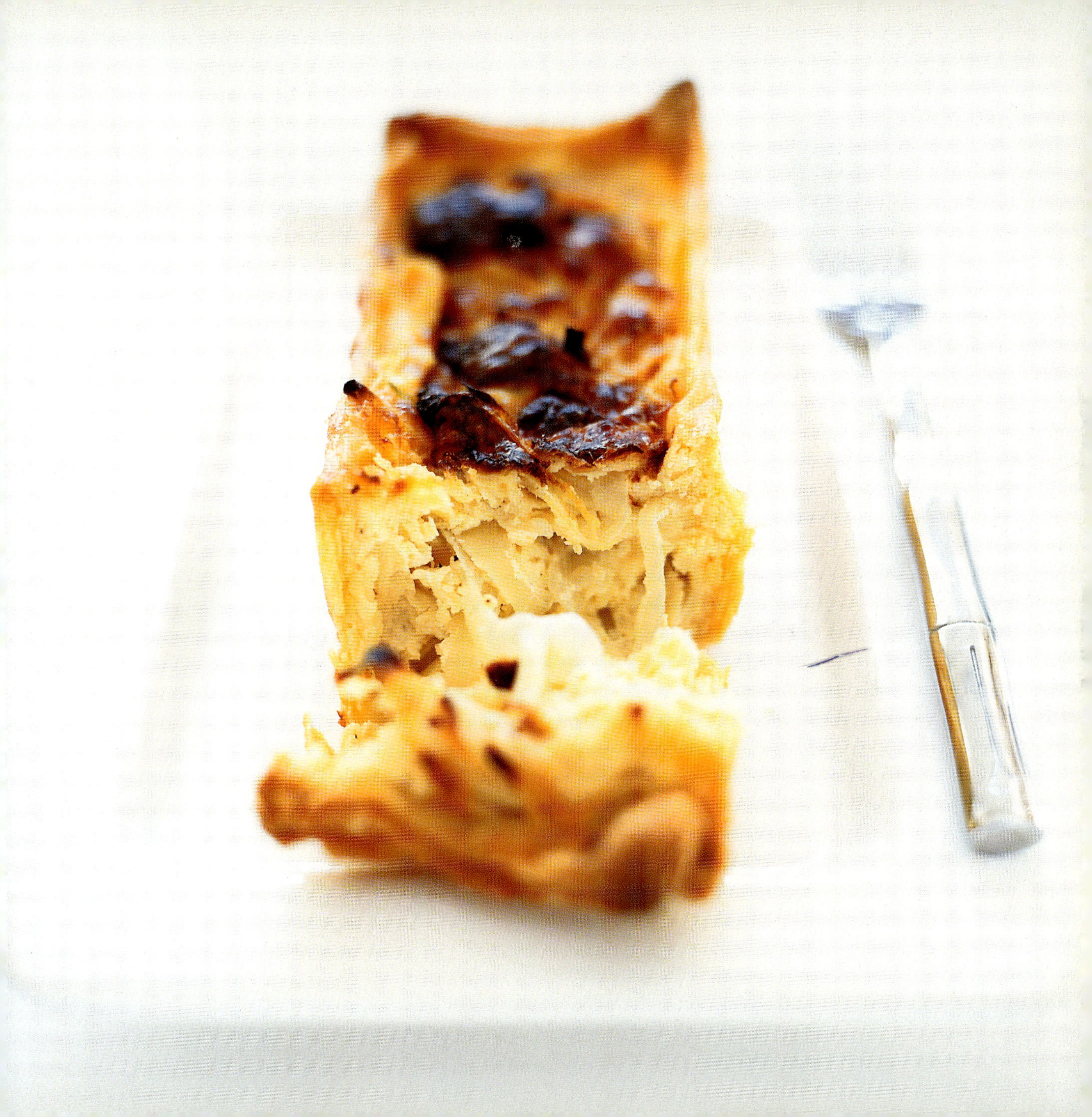

savory quiches

Mustard and cheese quiche

For the pie crust
2 cups all-purpose flour
pinch of salt
4 oz unsalted butter, diced
1 egg
1 teaspoon sour cream

For the filling
3 eggs
7 tablespoons milk
1 level cup sour cream
$^2/_3$ cup wholegrain mustard
1 cup grated cheese,
such as Gruyère
salt and pepper

To make the crust: put the flour and salt into a large bowl. Add the butter and with a knife cut it into the flour until evenly distributed, then use your fingertips to rub the fat lightly into the flour until the mixture resembles coarse crumbs. Whisk together the egg and sour cream and add gradually to the crumb mixture (you may not need to use all of it). Using a spatula or a knife, work the mixture together, then use your fingers until you have a smooth dough. Shape into a ball, put into a plastic bag and refrigerate for 1 hour before using.

Preheat the oven to 375°F. Lightly butter a removable bottom tart pan. Roll out the dough and use to line the pan. Prick all over with a fork. Refrigerate until needed.

To make the filling: in a bowl, whisk together the eggs, milk, and sour cream. Add the mustard and cheese and mix well. Season with salt and pepper.

Pour the batter into the crust shell and bake for about 40 minutes. Let cool slightly before serving.

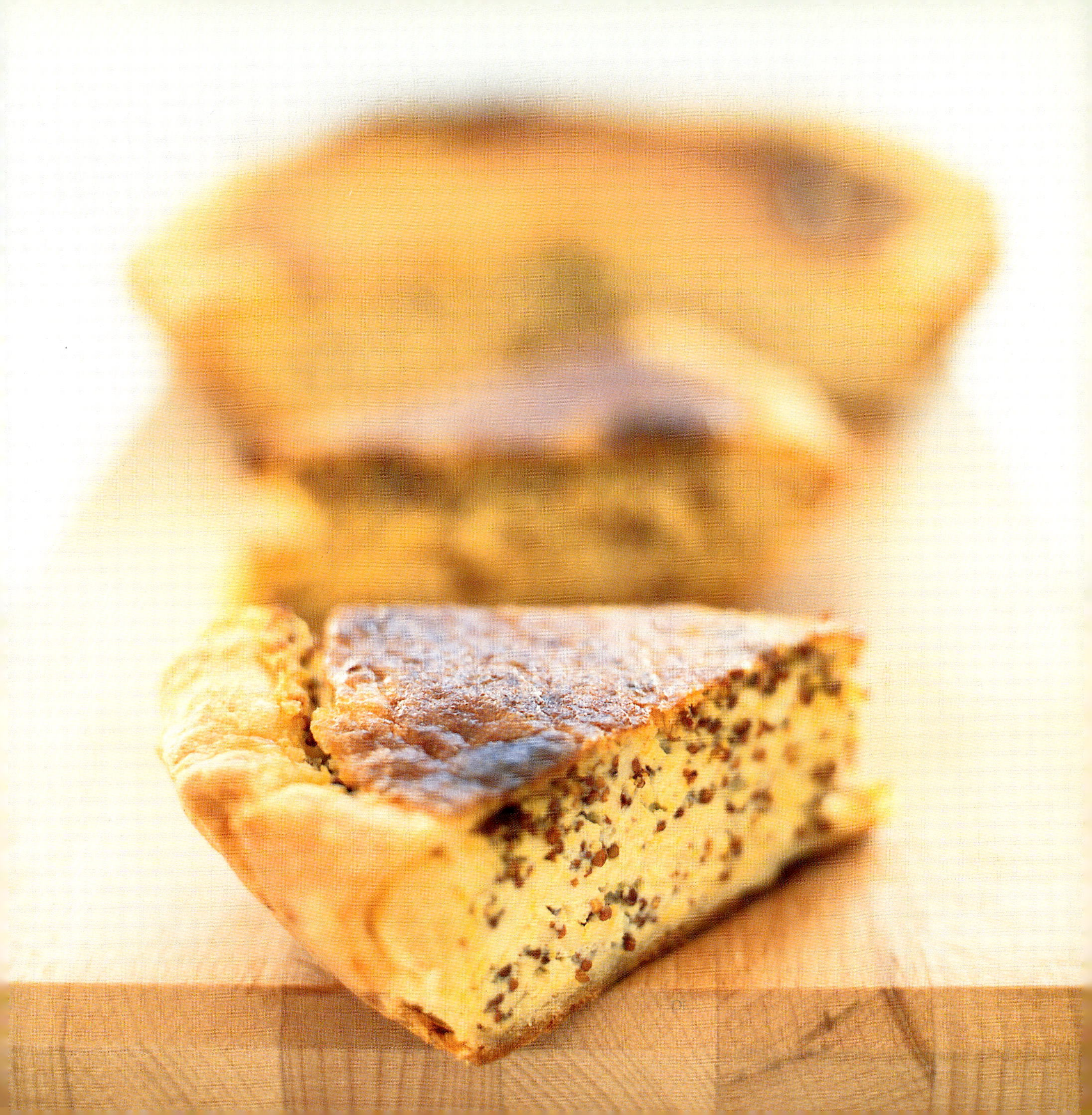

Spinach and ricotta quiche

For the pie crust
2 cups all-purpose flour
pinch of salt
4 oz unsalted butter, diced
1 egg
1 teaspoon sour cream

For the filling
1 lb fresh spinach
2 tablespoons unsalted butter
3 eggs
1 x 8 oz tub ricotta
½ level cup sour cream
pinch of freshly grated nutmeg
salt and pepper

To make the crust: put the flour and salt into a large bowl. Add the butter and with a knife cut it into the flour until evenly distributed, then use your fingertips to rub the fat lightly into the flour until the mixture resembles coarse crumbs. Whisk together the egg and sour cream and add gradually to the crumb mixture (you may not need to use all of it). Using a spatula or a knife, work the mixture together, then use your fingers until you have a smooth dough. Shape into a ball, put into a plastic bag and refrigerate for 1 hour before using.

Preheat the oven to 375°F. Lightly butter a removable bottom tart pan. Roll out the dough and use to line the pan. Prick all over with a fork. Refrigerate until needed.

To make the filling: wash the spinach, remove the stems and pat dry. Heat the butter in a large pan. Add the spinach and cook for about 8 minutes. Transfer to a colander, drain thoroughly, and squeeze out as much water as possible, then chop coarsely.

In a large bowl, whisk together the eggs, ricotta, and sour cream. Stir in the spinach. Season with nutmeg, salt, and pepper.

Pour into the crust shell and bake for about 40 minutes until firm and golden. Let cool slightly before serving.

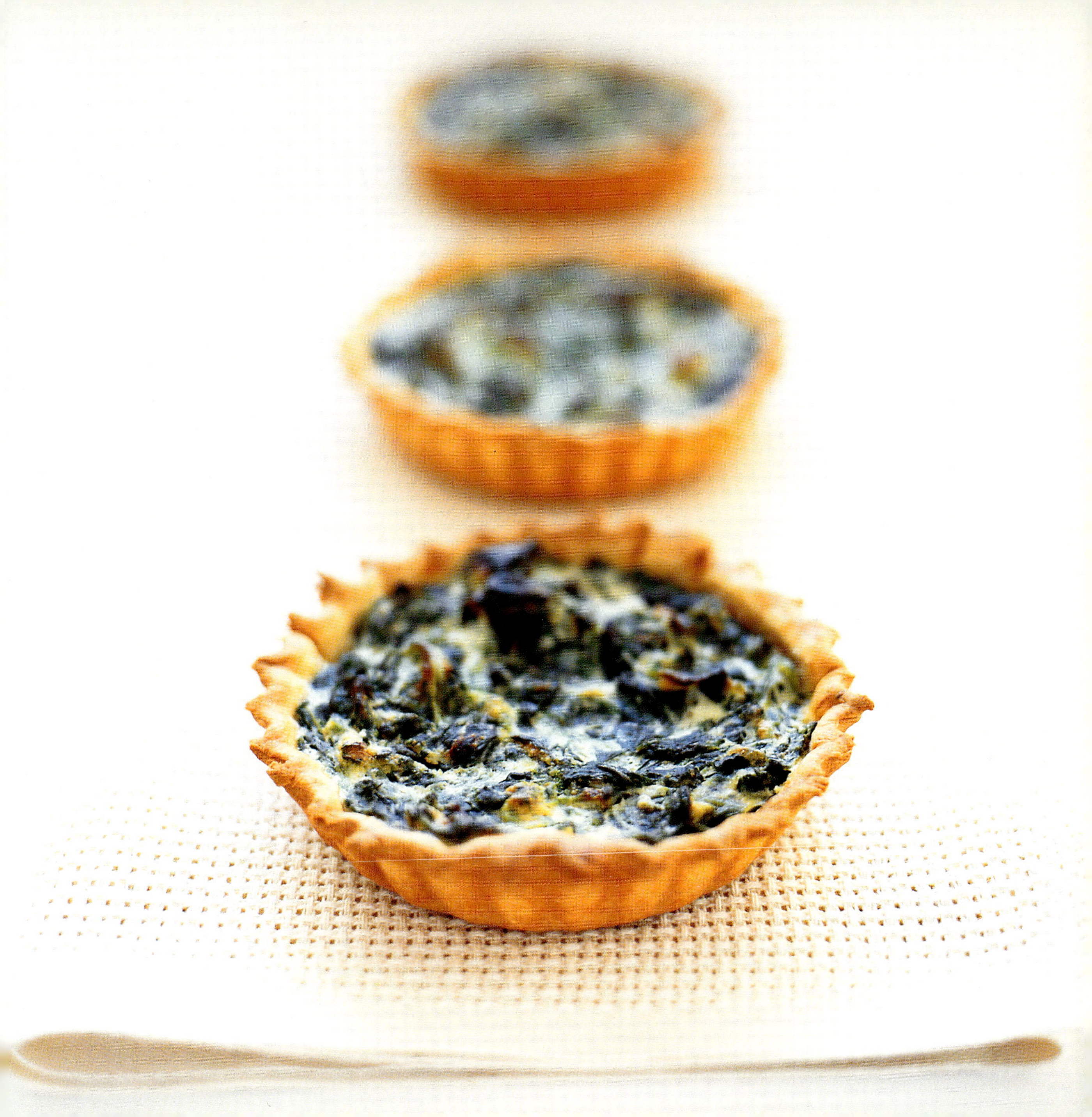

savory quiches

Munster cheese and bacon quiche

For the pie crust
2 cups all-purpose flour
pinch of salt
4 oz unsalted butter, diced
1 egg
1 teaspoon sour cream

For the filling
2 tablespoons unsalted butter
1½ cups coarsely chopped smoked bacon
3 onions, chopped
2 garlic cloves, crushed
3 tablespoons beer
1 level cup sour cream
8 oz Munster cheese, thinly sliced
small pinch of cumin seeds
salt and pepper

To make the crust: put the flour and salt into a large bowl. Add the butter and with a knife cut it into the flour until evenly distributed, then use your fingertips to rub the fat lightly into the flour until the mixture resembles coarse crumbs. Whisk together the egg and sour cream and add gradually to the crumb mixture (you may not need to use all of it). Using a spatula or a knife, work the mixture together, then use your fingers until you have a smooth dough. Shape into a ball, put into a plastic bag and refrigerate for 1 hour before using.

Preheat the oven to 375°F. Lightly butter a removable bottom tart pan. Roll out the dough and use to line the pan. Prick all over with a fork. Refrigerate until needed.

To make the filling: melt the butter in a skillet. Add the bacon and cook until browned. Add the onions and cook until golden. Add the garlic, beer, sour cream, and half of the cheese. Simmer gently for 3 minutes. Season with cumin seed, salt, and pepper.

Pour into the crust shell and top with the remaining slices of cheese. Bake for 20 minutes until golden.

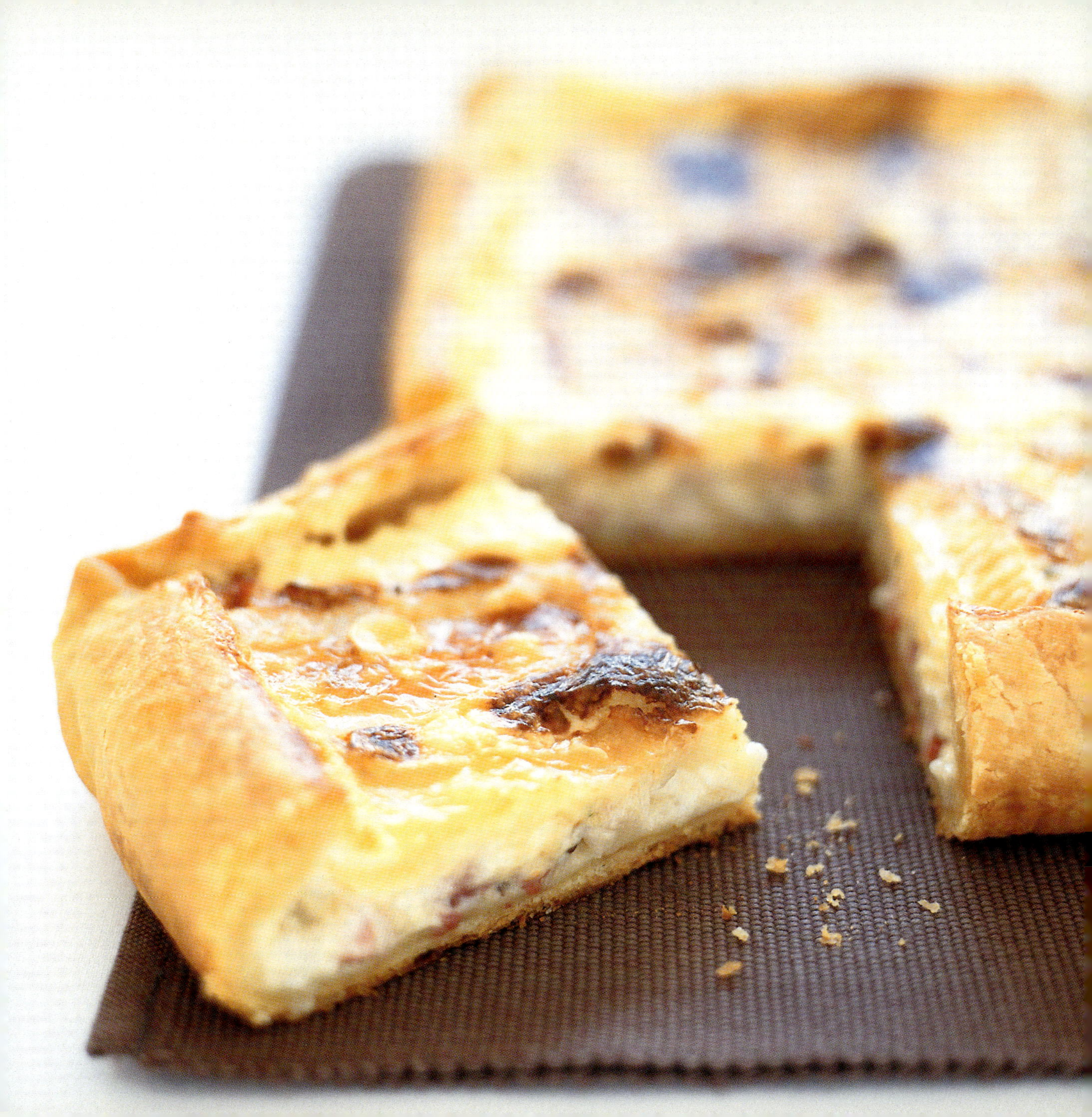

Tuna and vegetable quiche

For the pie crust
2 cups all-purpose flour
pinch of salt
4 oz unsalted butter, diced
1 egg
1 teaspoon sour cream

For the filling
oil
1 onion, chopped
2 garlic cloves, crushed
1 can peeled whole tomatoes, drained
pinch of dried thyme
4 eggs
1 can (9 oz) tuna in spring water, drained and flaked
1 cup peas, fresh or frozen
1 cup grated cheese, such as Gruyère
salt and pepper

To make the crust: put the flour and salt into a large bowl. Add the butter and with a knife cut it into the flour until evenly distributed, then use your fingertips to rub the fat lightly into the flour until the mixture resembles coarse crumbs. Whisk together the egg and sour cream and add gradually to the crumb mixture (you may not need to use all of it). Using a spatula or a knife, work the mixture together, then use your fingers until you have a smooth dough. Shape into a ball, put into a plastic bag and refrigerate for 1 hour before using.

Preheat the oven to 375°F. Lightly butter a removable bottom tart tin. Roll out the dough and use to line the pan. Prick all over with a fork. Refrigerate until needed.

To make the filling: heat some oil in a pan. Add the onion and garlic and cook until soft. Add the tomatoes and simmer gently for 20 minutes. Sprinkle with thyme, then set aside to cool.

Whisk the eggs in a large bowl. Stir in the tuna, peas, and tomato mixture. Season with salt and pepper. Pour into the crust shell, sprinkle with the cheese, and bake for about 45 minutes. Let cool slightly before serving.

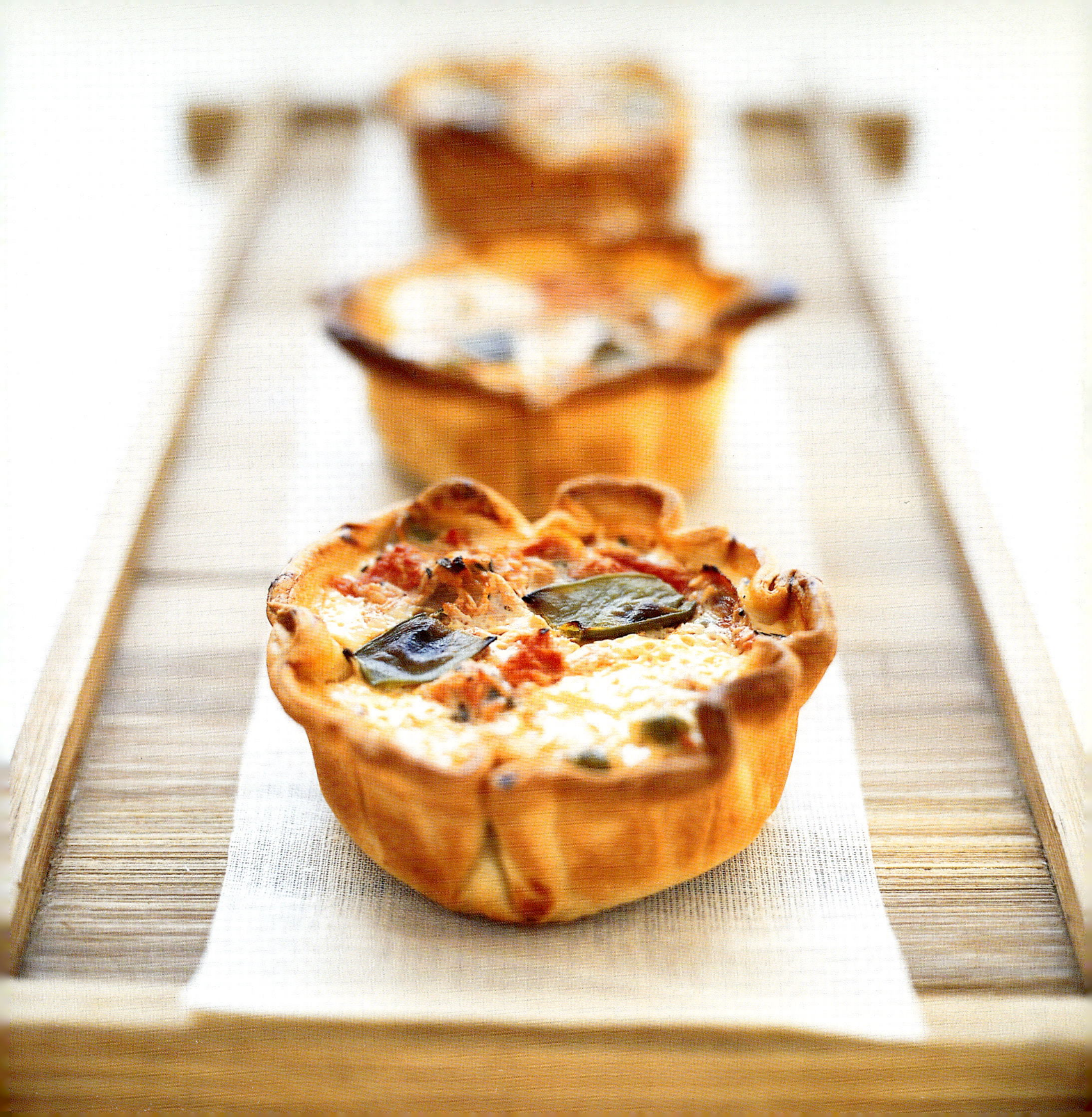

Feta cheese and fresh herb loaf

1½ cups all-purpose flour
3 teaspoons baking powder
3 eggs
7 tablespoons olive oil
1 tablespoon sunflower oil
7 tablespoons milk
7 oz feta cheese, cubed
1 cup grated cheese, such as Gruyère
2–3 handfuls of mixed fresh herbs
(basil, parsley, chives), chopped
salt and pepper

Preheat the oven to 350°F. Grease a loaf pan and dust lightly with flour.

In a large bowl, mix the flour and baking powder. In another bowl, whisk together the eggs, both oils, and the milk. Season with salt and pepper.

Pour the egg mixture into the flour mixture and fold in gently to combine. Stir in the feta, grated cheese, and fresh herbs.

Pour the batter into the prepared pan and bake for about 50 minutes, until the tip of a knife inserted in the center of the loaf comes out clean. Let cool in the pan before unmoulding.

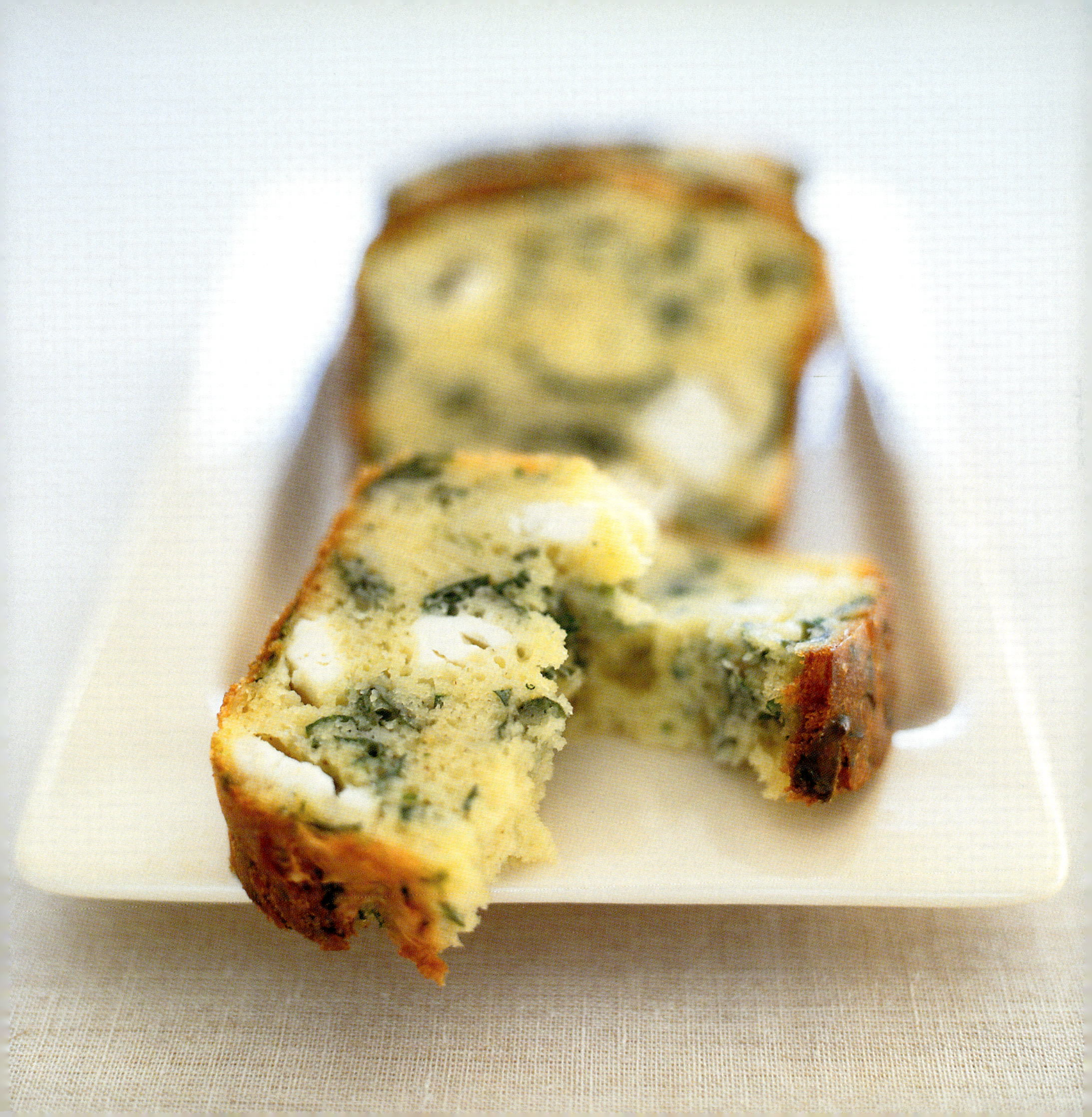

savory loaves

Parma ham and fig loaf

1½ cups all-purpose flour
3 teaspoons baking powder
3 eggs
7 tablespoons olive oil
7 tablespoons milk
1 cup grated cheese, such as Gruyère
7 oz fresh figs
3½ oz Parma ham, cut in strips
salt and pepper

Preheat the oven to 350°F. Grease a loaf pan and dust lightly with flour.

In a large bowl, mix the flour and baking powder. In another bowl, whisk together the eggs, oil, and the milk. Season with salt and pepper.

Pour the egg mixture into the flour mixture and fold in gently until there are no more lumps. Stir in the grated cheese, figs (whole or cut), and ham, and mix gently.

Pour the batter into the prepared pan and bake for about 50 minutes, until the tip of a knife inserted in the center of the loaf comes out clean. Let cool in the pan before unmoulding.

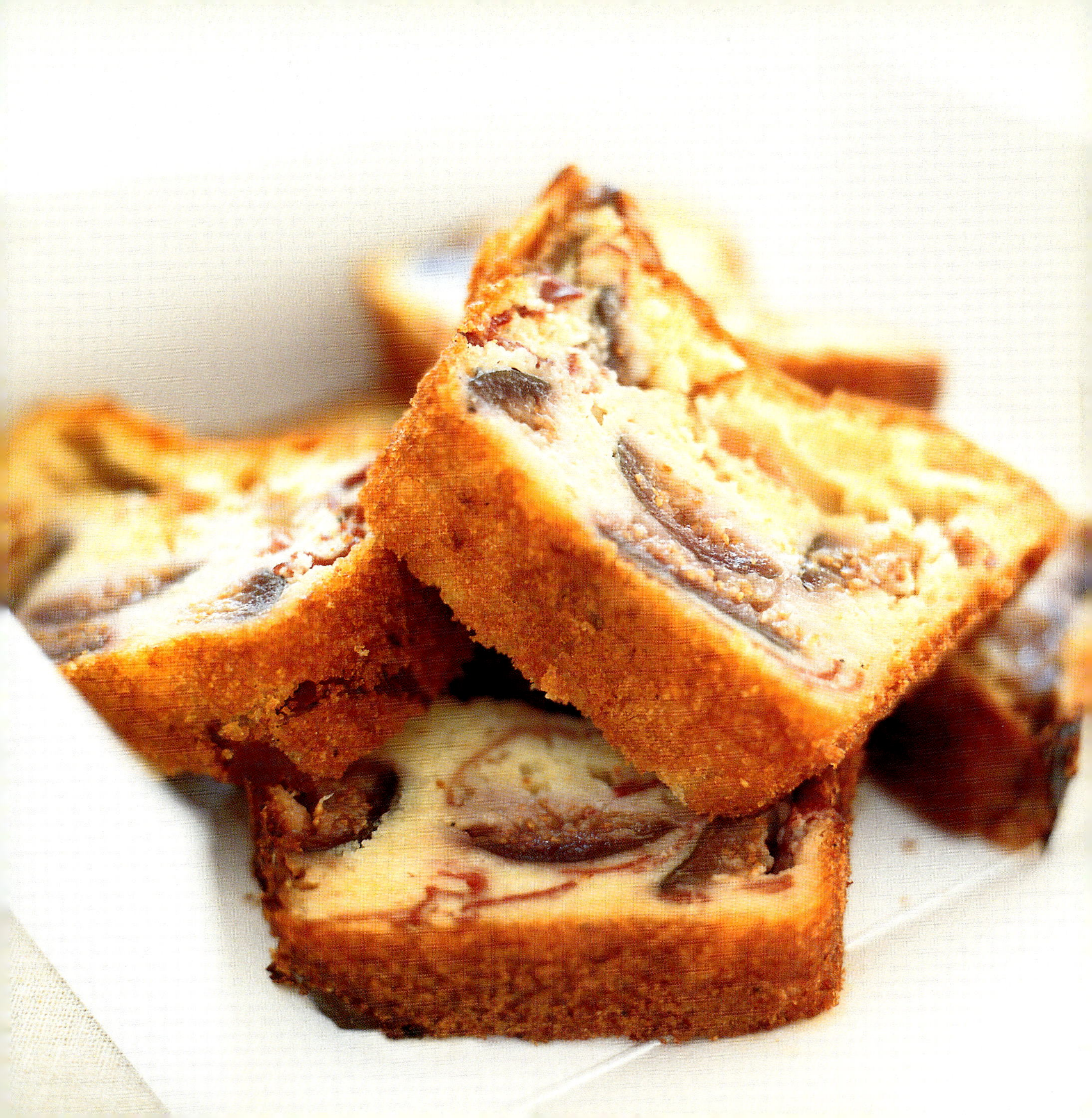

savory loaves

Roquefort, pear and walnut loaf

1½ cups all purpose flour
3 teaspoons baking powder
3 eggs
4 teaspoons walnut oil
7 tablespoons sunflower oil
7 tablespoons milk
1 cup grated cheese, such as Gruyère
crumbled Roquefort cheese
2 pears, peeled and cut into small cubes
1 cup walnut pieces
salt and pepper

Preheat the oven to 350°F. Grease a loaf pan and dust lightly with flour.

In a large bowl, mix the flour and baking powder. In another bowl, whisk together the eggs, both the oils, and the milk. Season with salt and pepper.

Pour the egg mixture into the flour mixture and fold in gently. Add the grated cheese and mix well. Stir in the Roquefort, pears, and walnut pieces until blended.

Pour the batter into the prepared pan and bake for about 50 minutes, until the tip of a knife inserted in the center of the loaf comes out clean. Let cool in the pan before unmoulding.

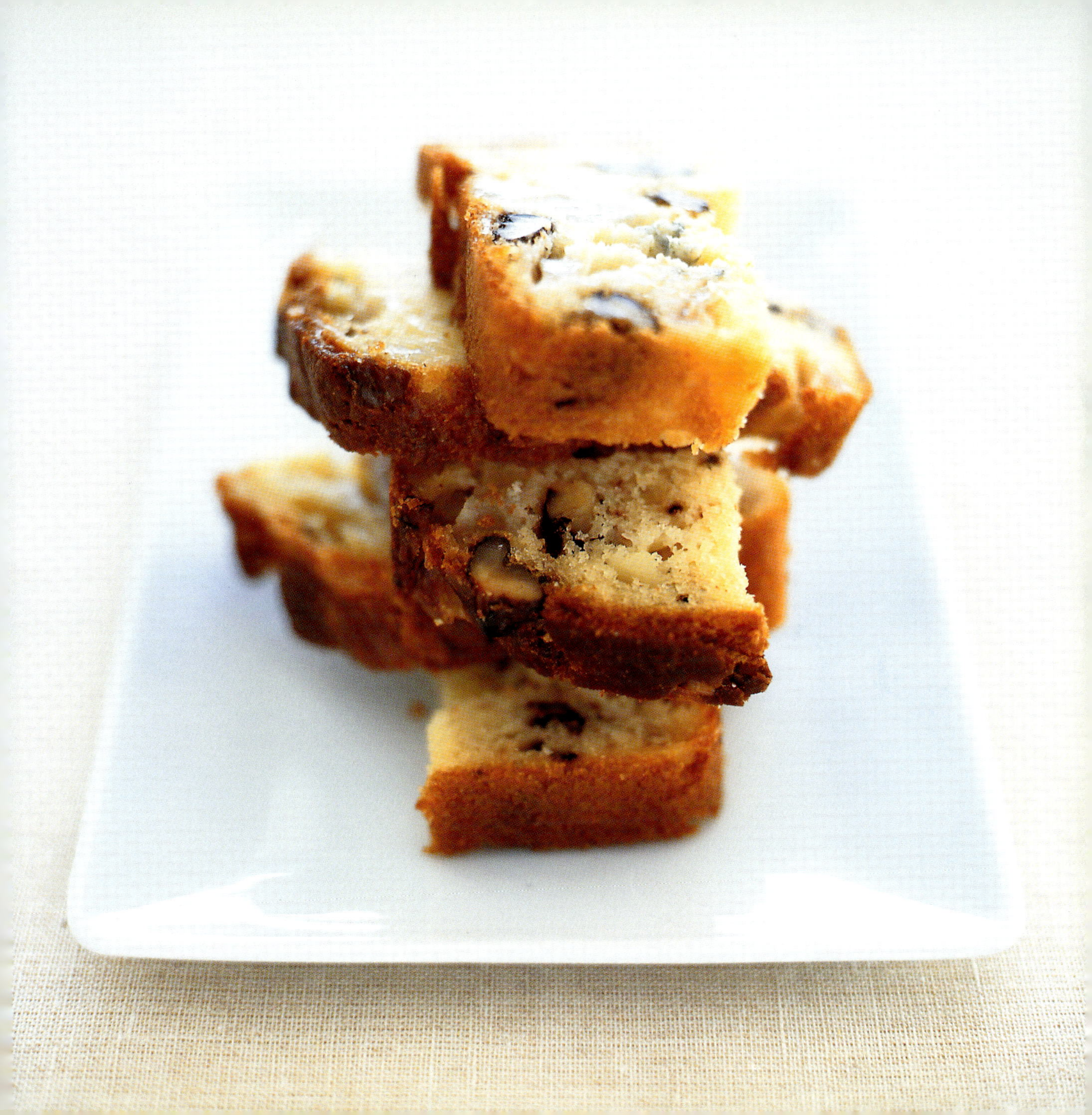

savory loaves

Mushroom loaf

unsalted butter
11 oz mixed mushrooms, sliced
2 shallots, chopped
1½ cups all-purpose flour
3 teaspoons baking powder
3 eggs
½ cup sunflower oil
7 tablespoons milk
1 cup grated cheese, such as Gruyère
1 handful of fresh parsley leaves, chopped
salt and pepper

Preheat the oven to 350°F. Grease a loaf pan and dust lightly with flour.

Heat a knob of butter in a pan, add the mushrooms and cook until all the liquid has evaporated. Add the shallots and cook for 1 minute more. Set aside to cool.

In a large bowl, mix the flour and baking powder. In another bowl, whisk together the eggs, oil, and the milk. Season with salt and pepper.

Pour the egg mixture into the flour mixture and fold in gently. Stir in the grated cheese and parsley. Add the mushroom mixture and mix to blend.

Pour the batter into the prepared pan and bake for about 50 minutes, until the tip of a knife inserted in the center of the loaf comes out clean. Let cool in the pan before unmoulding.

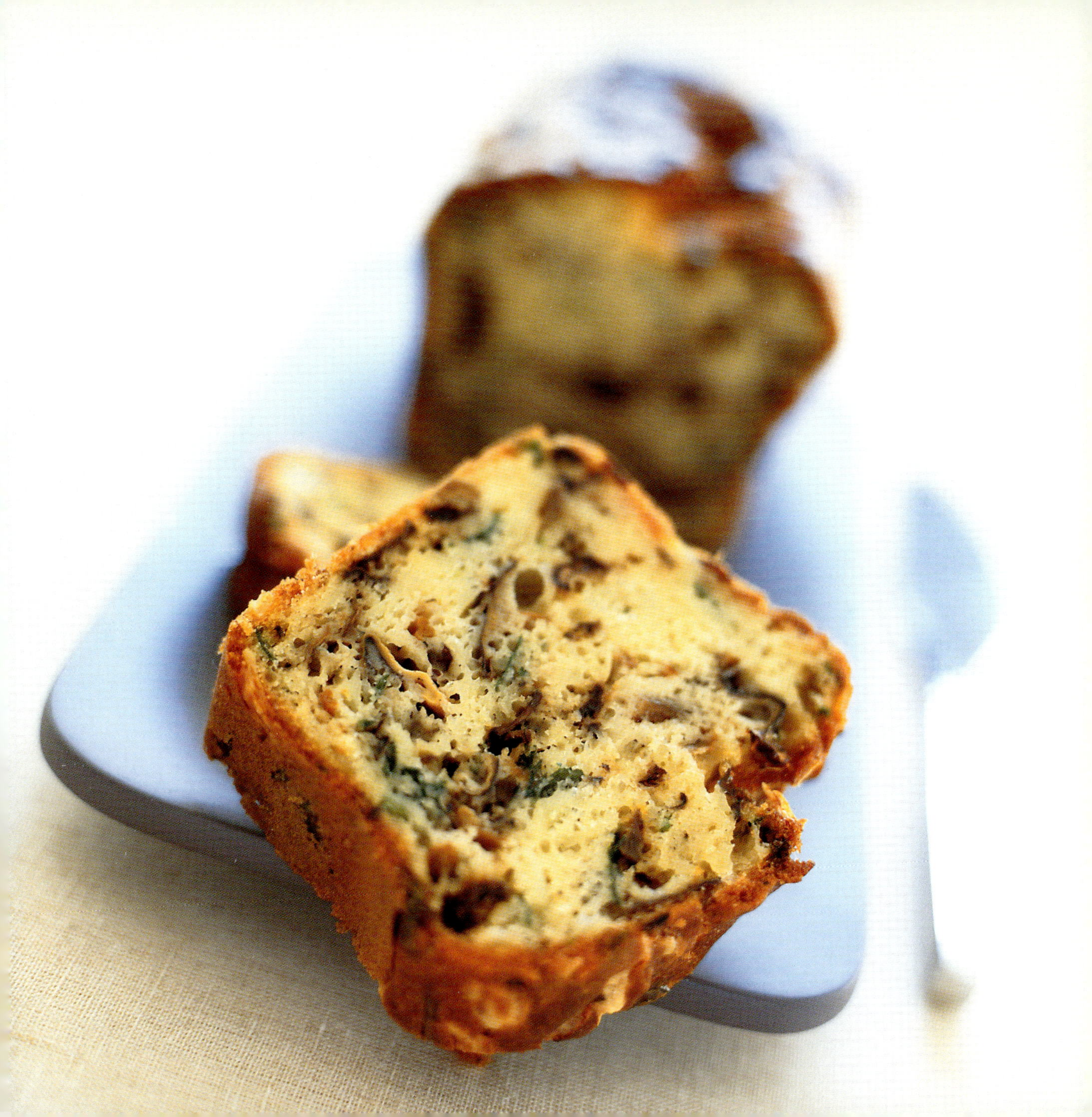

Zucchini and Parmesan loaf

8 oz zucchini
2 tablespoons unsalted butter
1½ cups all-purpose flour
3 teaspoons baking powder
3 eggs
3½ tablespoons sunflower oil
3½ tablespoons olive oil
7 tablespoons milk
1 cup grated cheese, such as Gruyère
1 cup grated Parmesan cheese
handful of basil leaves, chopped
handful of mint leaves, chopped
salt and pepper

Wash and dry the zucchini, then grate. Heat the butter in a pan. When melted, stir in the grated zucchini and cook until the liquid has evaporated.

Preheat the oven to 350°F. Grease a loaf pan and dust lightly with flour.

In a large bowl, mix the flour and baking powder. In another bowl, whisk together the eggs, both oils, and the milk. Season with salt and pepper.

Pour the egg mixture into the flour mixture and fold in gently. Stir in the grated cheese, Parmesan, basil, mint, and zucchini. Mix well.

Pour the batter into the prepared pan and bake for about 50 minutes, until the tip of a knife inserted in the center of the loaf comes out clean. Let cool in the pan before unmoulding.

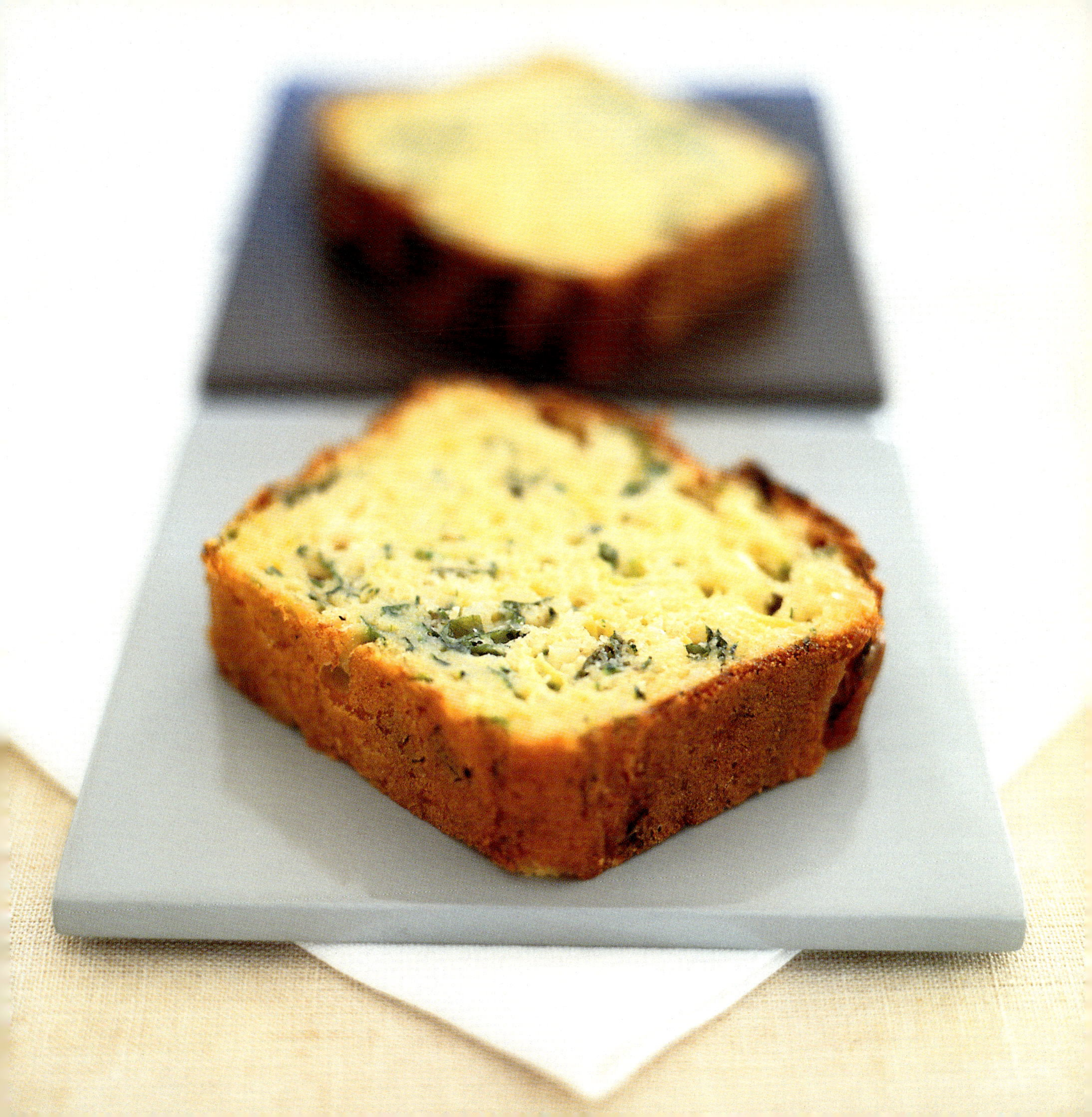

Green and black olive loaf

1½ cups all-purpose flour
3 teaspoons baking powder
3 eggs
7 tablespoons olive oil
7 tablespoons milk
1 cup grated cheese, such as Gruyère
3½ oz hickory smoked bacon,
cut into strips
⅔ cup green olives, stoned
⅔ cup black olives, stoned
salt and pepper

Preheat the oven to 350°F. Grease a loaf pan and dust lightly with flour.

In a large bowl, mix the flour and baking powder. In another bowl, whisk together the eggs, oil, and the milk. Season with salt and pepper.

Pour the egg mixture into the flour mixture and fold in gently. Stir in the grated cheese, bacon, and all the olives.

Pour the batter into the prepared pan and bake for about 50 minutes, until the tip of a knife inserted in the center of the loaf comes out clean. Let cool in the pan before unmoulding.

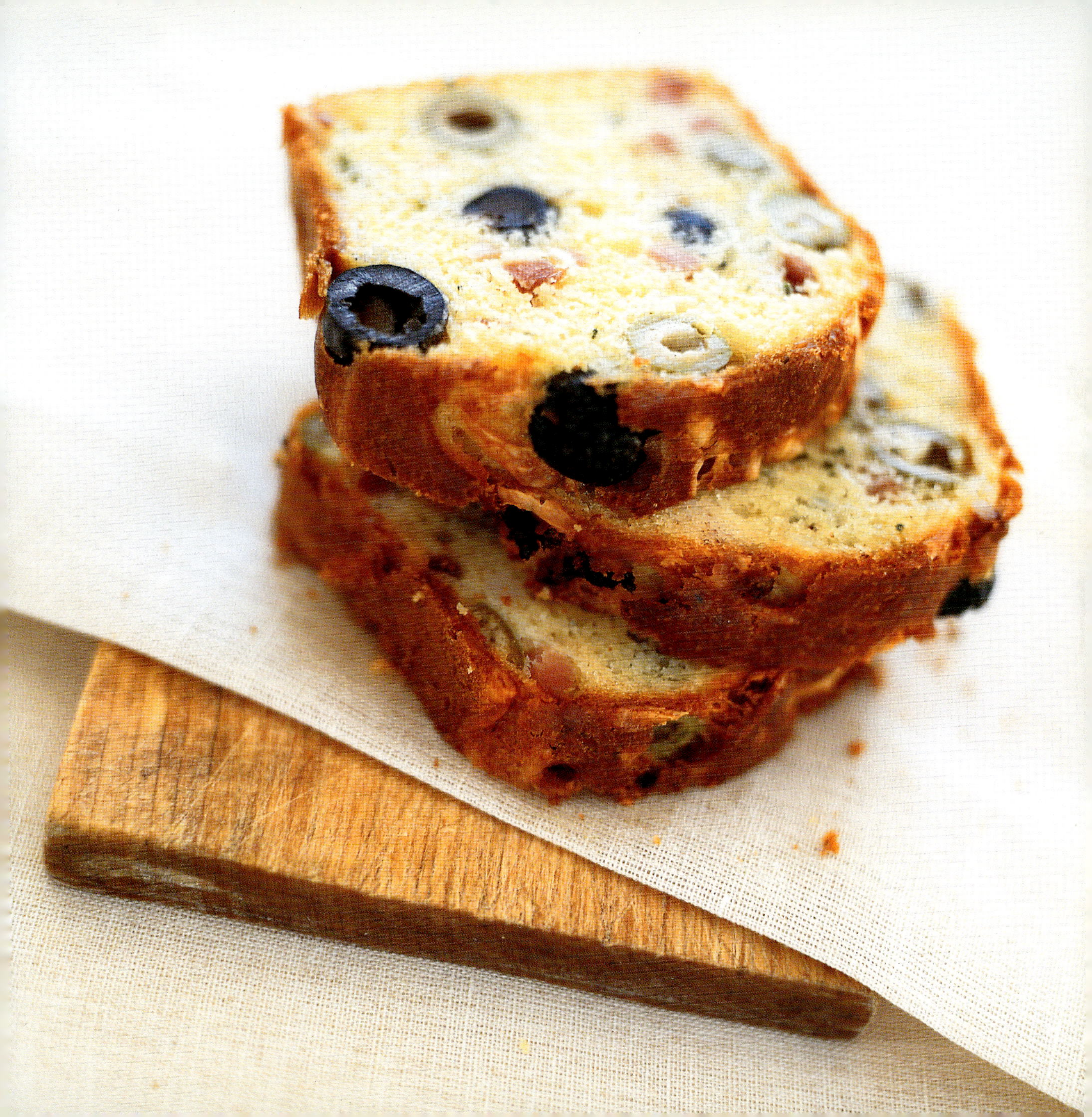

savory loaves

Bacon, sausage and cheese loaf

1⅓ cups all-purpose flour
3 teaspoons baking powder
3 eggs
7 tablespoons walnut oil
7 tablespoons milk
1 cup grated cheese, such as Gruyère
5 oz hickory smoked bacon, cut into strips
100 g (3½ oz) French-style saucisson
(or other well-flavored sausage), chopped
salt and pepper

Preheat the oven to 350°F. Grease a loaf pan and dust lightly with flour.

In a large bowl, mix the flour and baking powder. In another bowl, whisk together the eggs, oil, and the milk. Season with salt and pepper.

Pour the egg mixture into the flour mixture and fold in gently until there are no more lumps. Stir in the grated cheese, bacon, and saucisson. Mix well.

Pour the batter into the prepared pan and bake for about 50 minutes, until the tip of a knife inserted in the center of the loaf comes out clean. Let cool in the pan before unmoulding.

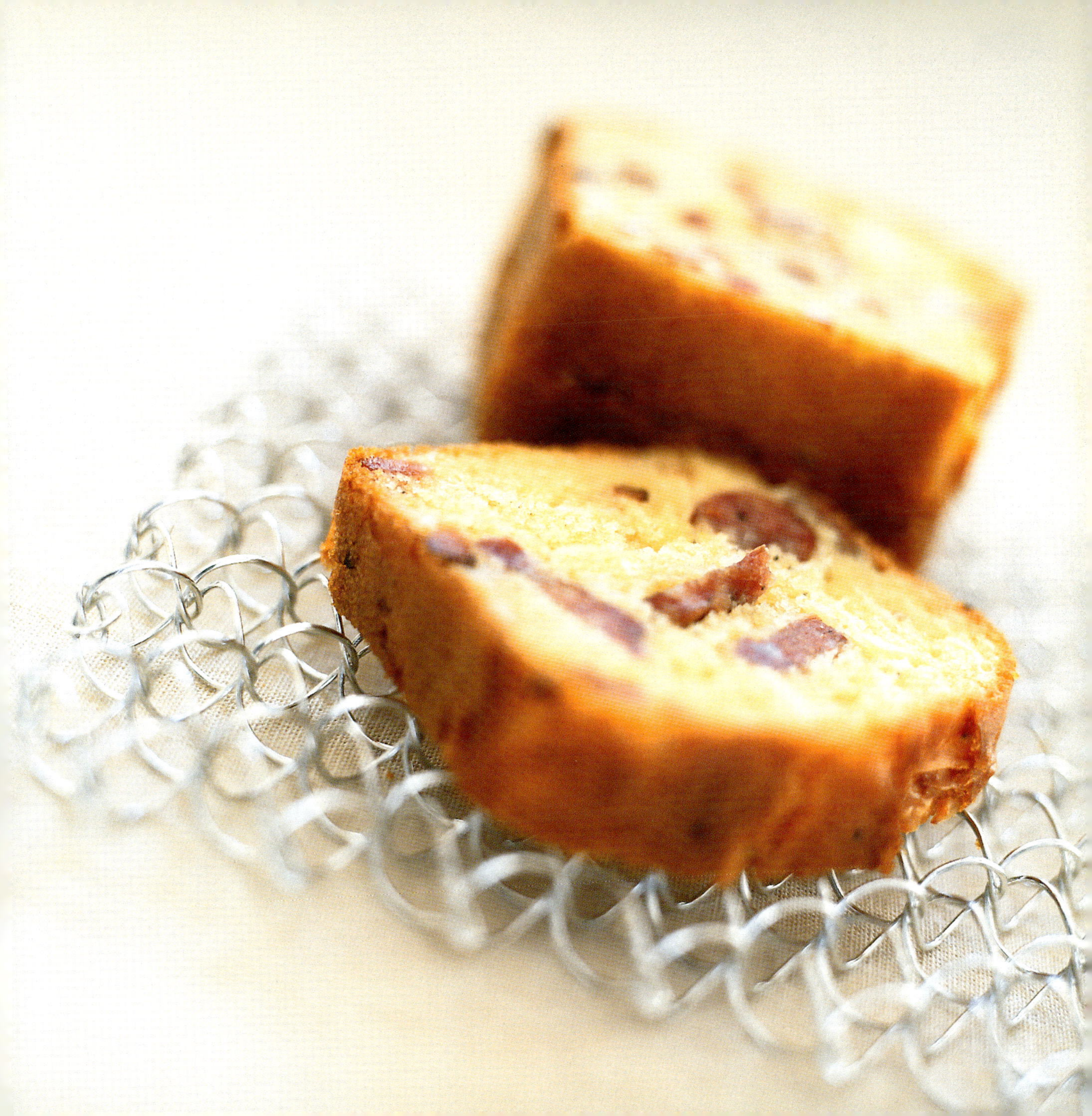

Salmon, dill and pink peppercorn loaf

2 tablespoons unsalted butter
8 oz salmon, smoked or fresh
1½ cups all-purpose flour
3 teaspoons baking powder
3 eggs
7 tablespoons sunflower oil
7 tablespoons milk
1 cup grated cheese, such as Gruyère
handful of fresh dill, chopped
2 pinches pink peppercorns, crushed
salt and pepper

Melt the butter in a pan. Cut the salmon into pieces and cook in the butter for around 5 minutes.

Preheat the oven to 350°F. Grease a loaf pan and dust lightly with flour.

In a large bowl, mix the flour and baking powder. In another bowl, whisk together the eggs, oil, and the milk. Season with salt and pepper.

Pour the egg mixture into the flour mixture and fold in gently until there are no more lumps. Stir in the grated cheese, salmon, dill, and pink peppercorns. Mix well.

Pour the batter into the prepared pan and bake for about 50 minutes, until the tip of a knife inserted in the center of the loaf comes out clean. Let cool in the pan before unmoulding.

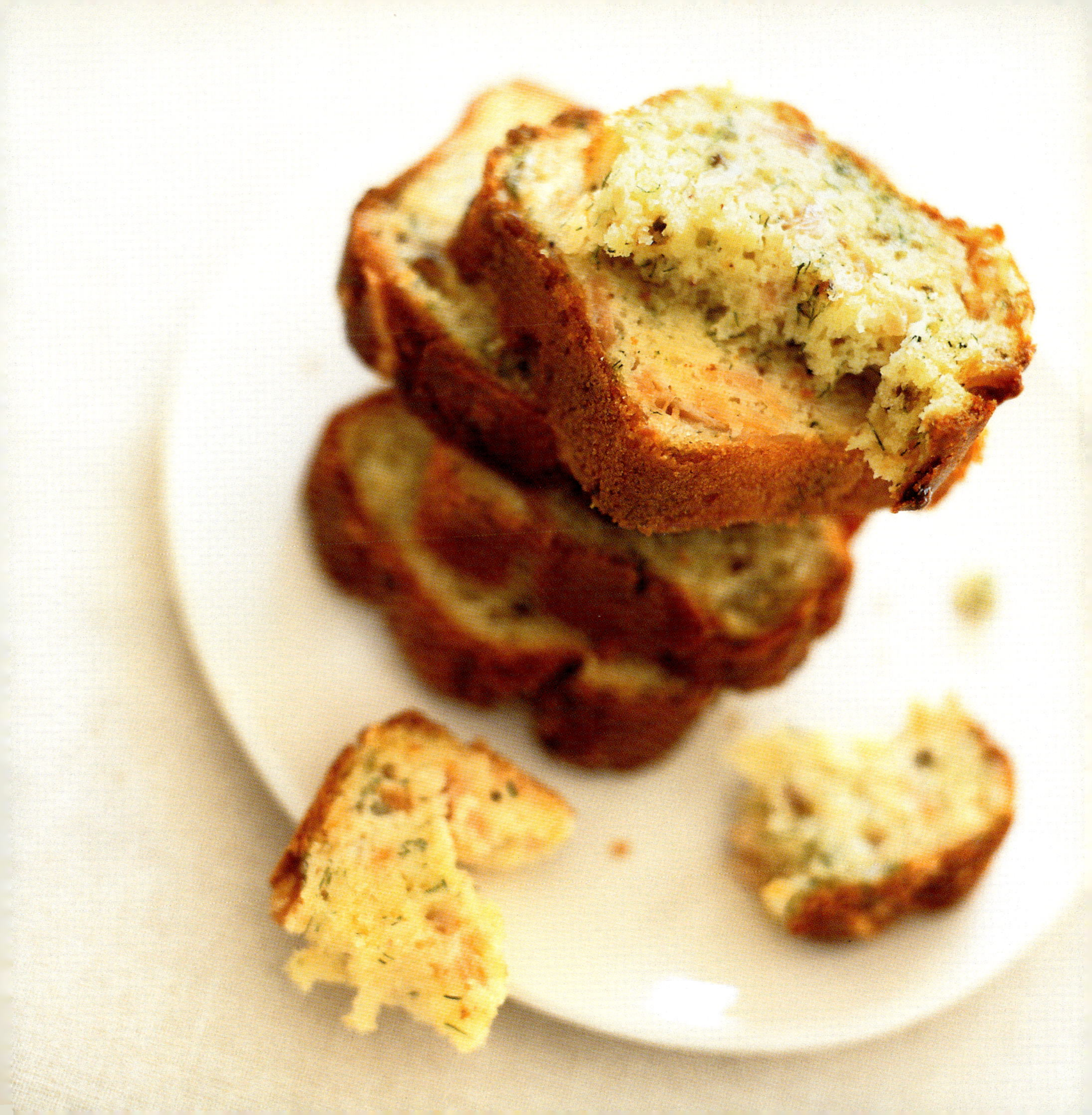

Sun-dried tomato, caper and basil loaf

1½ cups all-purpose flour
3 teaspoons baking powder
3 eggs
7 tablespoons olive oil
7 tablespoons milk
1 cup grated cheese, such as Gruyère
7 oz sun-dried tomatoes, chopped
2 tablespoons capers in salt, rinsed
large handful of fresh basil leaves, torn by hand into small pieces, or snipped with scissors
salt and pepper

Preheat the oven to 350°F. Grease a loaf pan and dust lightly with flour.

In a large bowl, mix the flour and baking powder. In another bowl, whisk together the eggs, oil, and the milk. Season with salt and pepper.

Pour the egg mixture into the flour mixture and fold in gently until there are no more lumps. Stir in the grated cheese, sun-dried tomatoes, capers, and basil. Mix well.

Pour the batter into the prepared pan and bake for about 45 minutes, until the tip of a knife inserted in the center of the loaf comes out clean. Let cool in the pan before unmoulding.

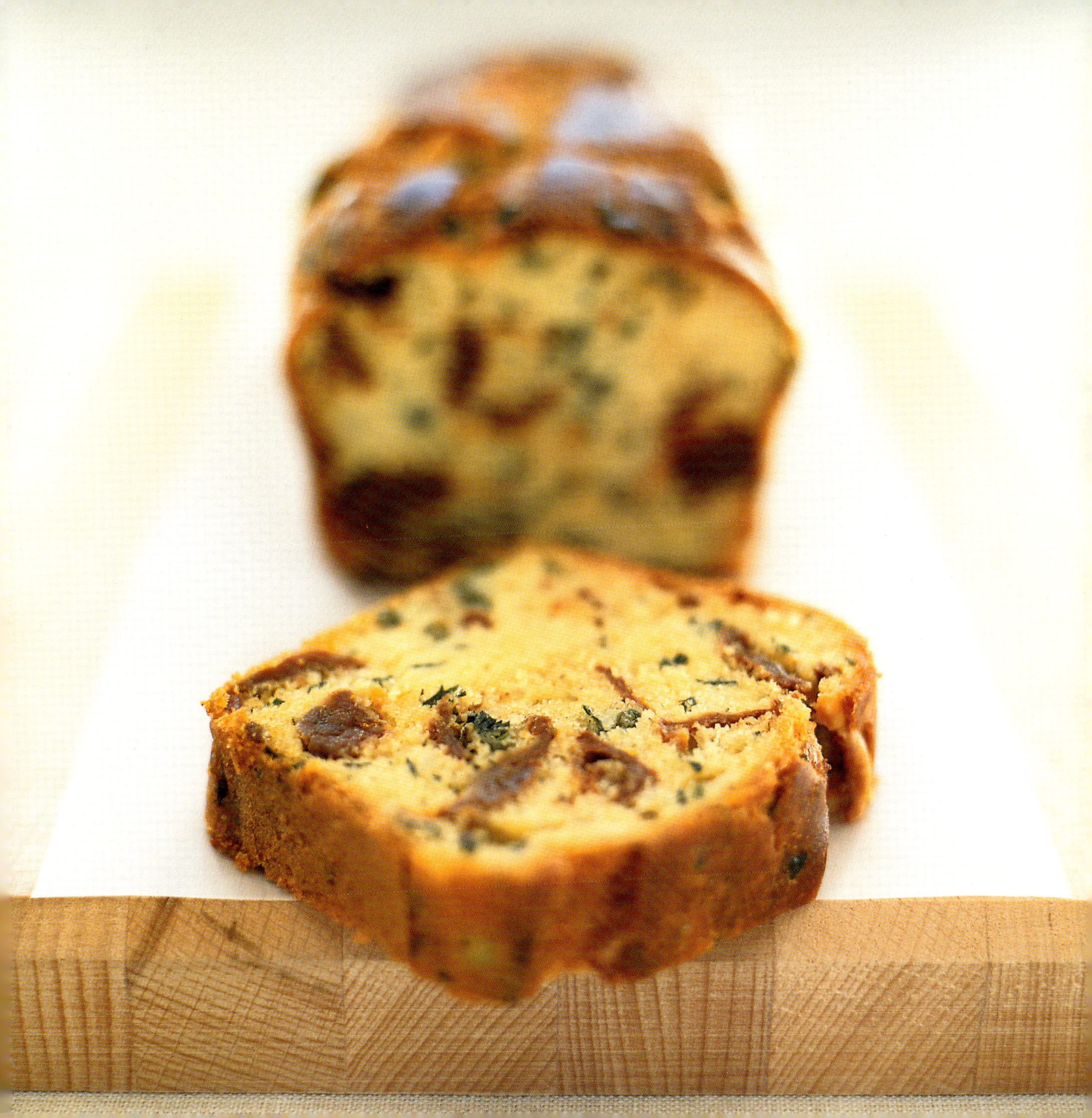

Pesto and pine nut loaf

1½ cups all-purpose flour
3 teaspoons baking powder
3 eggs
3 tablespoons olive oil
7 tablespoons milk
1 cup grated cheese, such as Gruyère
5 oz pesto (see below)
large handful of pine nuts
salt and pepper

For the pesto
3 large bunches of basil
3 garlic cloves
½ cup pine nuts
4 tablespoons grated Parmesan cheese
7 tablespoons olive oil
coarse salt

To make the pesto: combine the basil leaves, garlic, pine nuts, and a pinch of coarse salt in a food processor and blend until smooth. Transfer to a bowl and carefully stir in the Parmesan and oil with a fork.

Preheat the oven to 350°F. Grease a loaf pan and dust lightly with flour.

In a large bowl, mix the flour and baking powder. In another bowl, whisk together the eggs, oil, and the milk. Season with salt and pepper.

Pour the egg mixture into the flour mixture and fold in gently until there are no more lumps. Stir in the grated cheese, pesto, and whole pine nuts. Mix well.

Pour the batter into the prepared pan and bake for about 50 minutes, until the tip of a knife inserted in the center of the loaf comes out clean. Let cool in the pan before unmoulding.

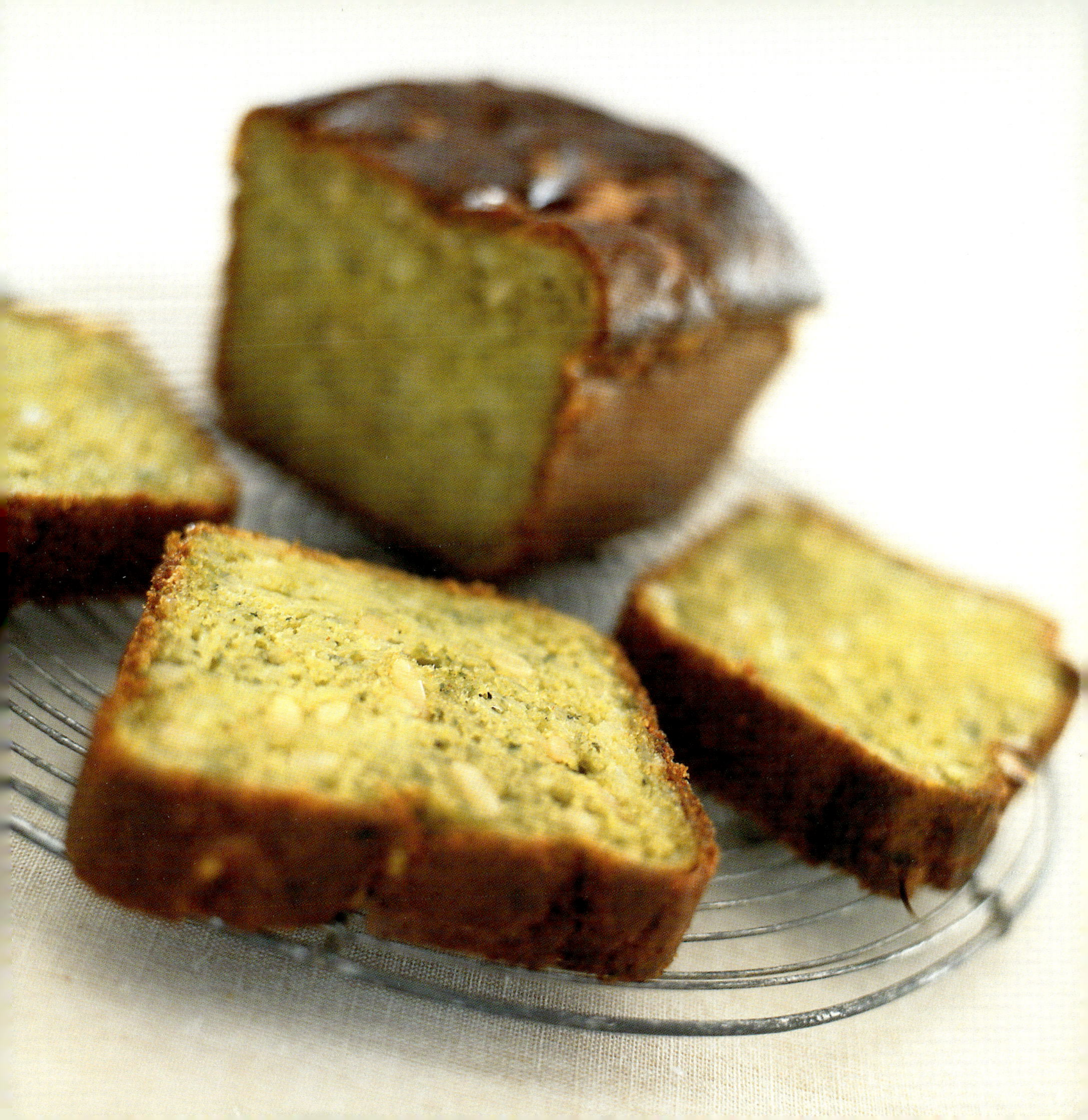

sweet tarts

Strawberry and rhubarb tart

For the sweet pie crust
2 cups all-purpose flour
5½ tablespoons superfine sugar
pinch of salt
4 oz unsalted butter
1 egg
1 teaspoon sour cream

For the filling
1 lb rhubarb
2 tablespoons unsalted butter
¾ cup superfine sugar
7 oz strawberries, trimmed and halved
¾ cup sour cream

To make the crust: put the flour, sugar and salt into a large bowl. Add the butter and with a knife cut it into the flour until evenly distributed, then use your fingertips to rub the fat lightly into the flour until the mixture resembles coarse crumbs. Whisk together the egg and sour cream and add gradually to the crumb mixture (you may not need all of it). Using a spatula or a knife, work the mixture together, then use your fingers until you have a smooth dough. Shape into a ball, put into a plastic bag and refrigerate for 1 hour before using.

Preheat the oven to 375°F. Lightly butter a removable bottom tart pan. Roll out the dough and use to line the pan. Prick the base with a fork. To bake blind: cover the crust with a round of baking parchment and weight with dry beans or pie weights. Bake for 20 minutes. Remove from the oven and take out the weights. Set aside.

To make the filling: Trim the rhubarb and cut into pieces. In a pan, combine the butter, sugar, and rhubarb pieces over low heat and cook until tender. Remove from the heat and stir in the strawberries and sour cream.

Spread the rhubarb and strawberry batter in the prebaked tart shell and bake for 20 minutes until golden.

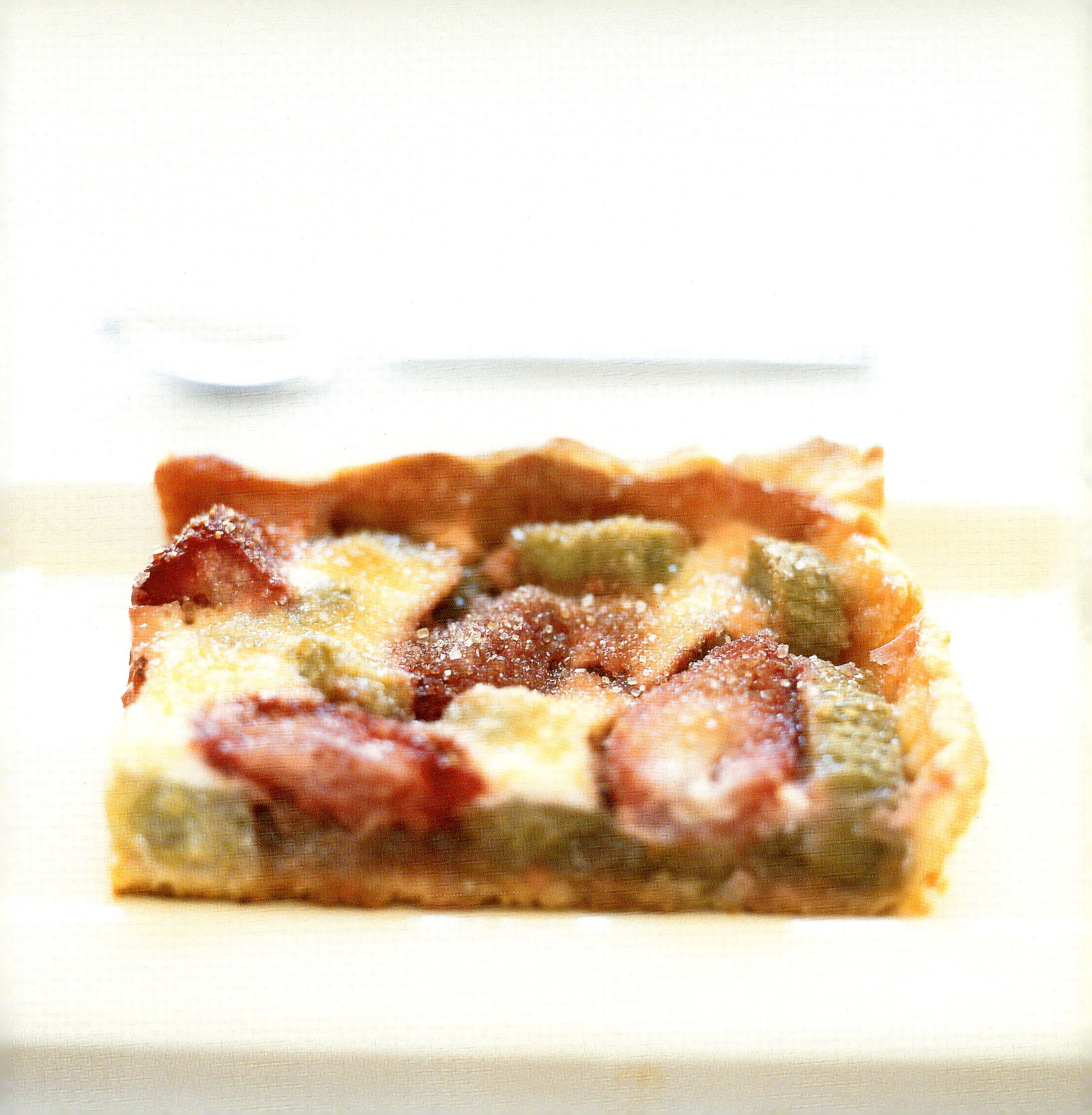

Dark chocolate tart

For the sweet pie crust
2 cups all-purpose flour
5½ tablespoons superfine sugar
pinch of salt
4 oz unsalted butter
1 egg
1 teaspoon sour cream

For the filling
11 oz bittersweet chocolate (not unsweetened), or dark European chocolate (at least 70% chocolate solids)
1¼ cups whipping cream
3 oz unsalted butter, cut in pieces
3 eggs and 3 egg yolks
3 tablespoons superfine sugar

To make the crust: put the flour, sugar, and salt into a large bowl. Add the butter and with a knife cut it into the flour until evenly distributed, then use your fingertips to rub the fat lightly into the flour until the mixture resembles coarse crumbs. Whisk together the egg and sour cream and add gradually to the crumb mixture (you may not need all of it). Using a spatula or a knife, work the mixture together, then use your fingers until you have a smooth dough. Shape into a ball, put into a plastic bag and refrigerate for 1 hour before using.

Preheat the oven to 375°F. Lightly butter a removable bottom tart pan. Roll out the dough and use to line the pan. Prick the base with a fork. To bake blind: cover the crust with a round of baking parchment and weight with dry beans or pie weights. Bake for 20 minutes. Remove from the oven and take out the weights. Set aside.

To make the filling: Cut the chocolate into very small pieces. Bring the cream to a boil in a pan. Remove from the heat and stir in the chocolate and butter until completely melted. In another bowl, whisk together the eggs, egg yolks, and sugar. When the chocolate mixture has cooled, stir in the egg mixture.

Lower the oven to 300°F. Pour the chocolate batter into the prebaked tart shell and bake for 20 minutes. Let cool before serving.

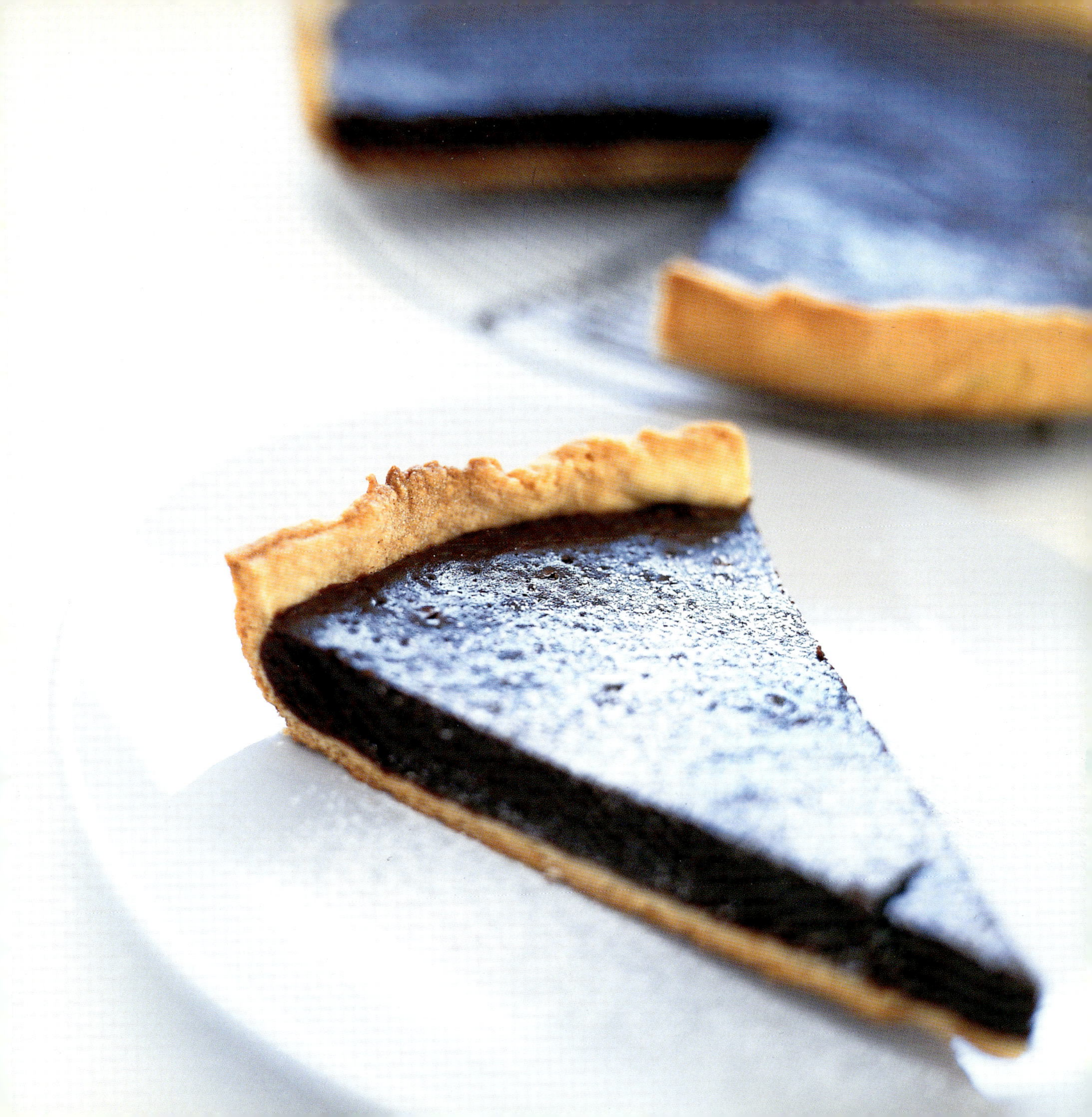

sweet tarts

Tarte Tatin

For the pie crust
2 cups all-purpose flour
pinch of salt
4 oz unsalted butter
1 egg
1 teaspoon sour cream

For the filling
1¾ lb apples
2 oz unsalted butter
7½ tablespoons superfine sugar
pinch of ground cinnamon

To make the crust: put the flour and salt into a large bowl. Add the butter and with a knife cut it into the flour until evenly distributed, then use your fingertips to rub the fat lightly into the flour until the mixture resembles coarse crumbs. Whisk together the egg and sour cream and add gradually to the crumb mixture (you may not need all of it). Using a spatula or a knife, work the mixture together, then use your fingers until you have a smooth dough. Shape into a ball, put into a plastic bag and refrigerate for 1 hour before using.

Preheat the oven to 400°F.

To make the filling: peel, core, and quarter the apples. Melt the butter in a flameproof pie dish over low heat. Sprinkle a thin layer of sugar over the bottom and add the cinnamon. Stir until the sugar melts and begins to caramelize. Remove from the heat.

Arrange the apple quarters in the dish, working from the outside edge into the center, until filled. Sprinkle with the remaining sugar and bake for 5–10 minutes.

Roll out the dough and place on top of the apples. Push down gently, then prick all over with a fork. Bake for 25–30 minutes. Remove from the oven and let rest for 2 minutes. Unmould upside down onto a plate, so that the apples are on top. Serve warm, with sour cream.

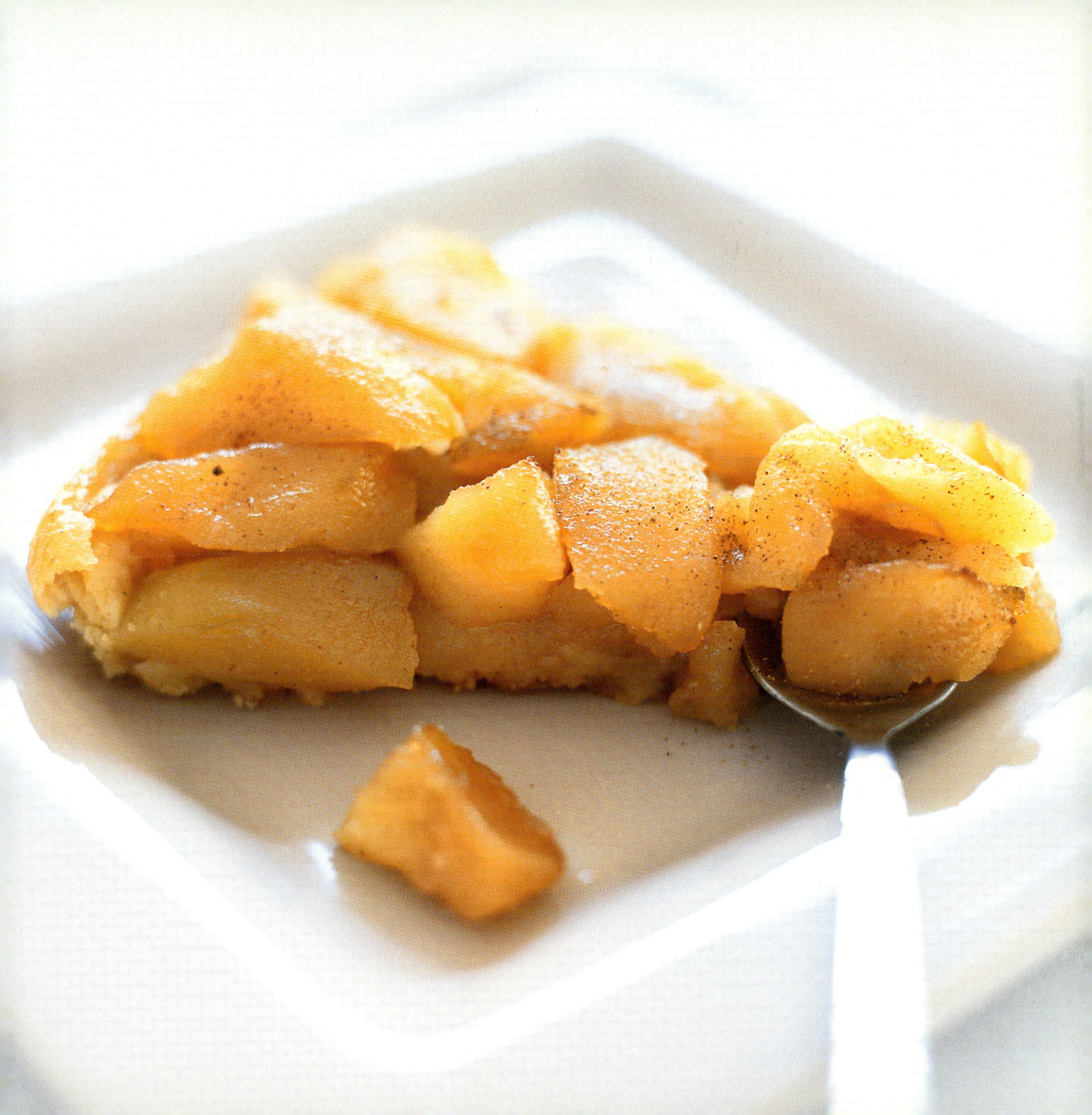

Raspberry conserve tart

For the sweet pie crust
3 1/8 cups all-purpose flour
1/2 cup superfine sugar
pinch of salt
7 oz unsalted butter
2 eggs
1 tablespoon sour cream

For the filling
12 oz raspberry conserve
(any red fruit conserve will work: cherry, strawberry, redcurrant)

To make the crust: put the flour, sugar, and salt into a large bowl. Add the butter and with a knife cut it into the flour until evenly distributed, then use your fingertips to rub the fat lightly into the flour until the mixture resembles coarse crumbs. Whisk together the egg and sour cream and add gradually to the crumb mixture (you may not need all of it). Using a spatula or a knife, work the mixture together, then use your fingers until you have a smooth dough. Shape into a ball, put into a plastic bag and refrigerate for 1 hour before using.

Preheat the oven to 350°F. Lightly butter a removable bottom tart pan. Roll out the dough and use to line the pan. Roll out the leftover dough and cut into thin strips. Prick the dough in the pan all over with a fork.

Spread the raspberry conserve in the crust shell and lay the dough strips on top, in a trellis pattern.

Bake for 40 minutes. Let cool before serving.

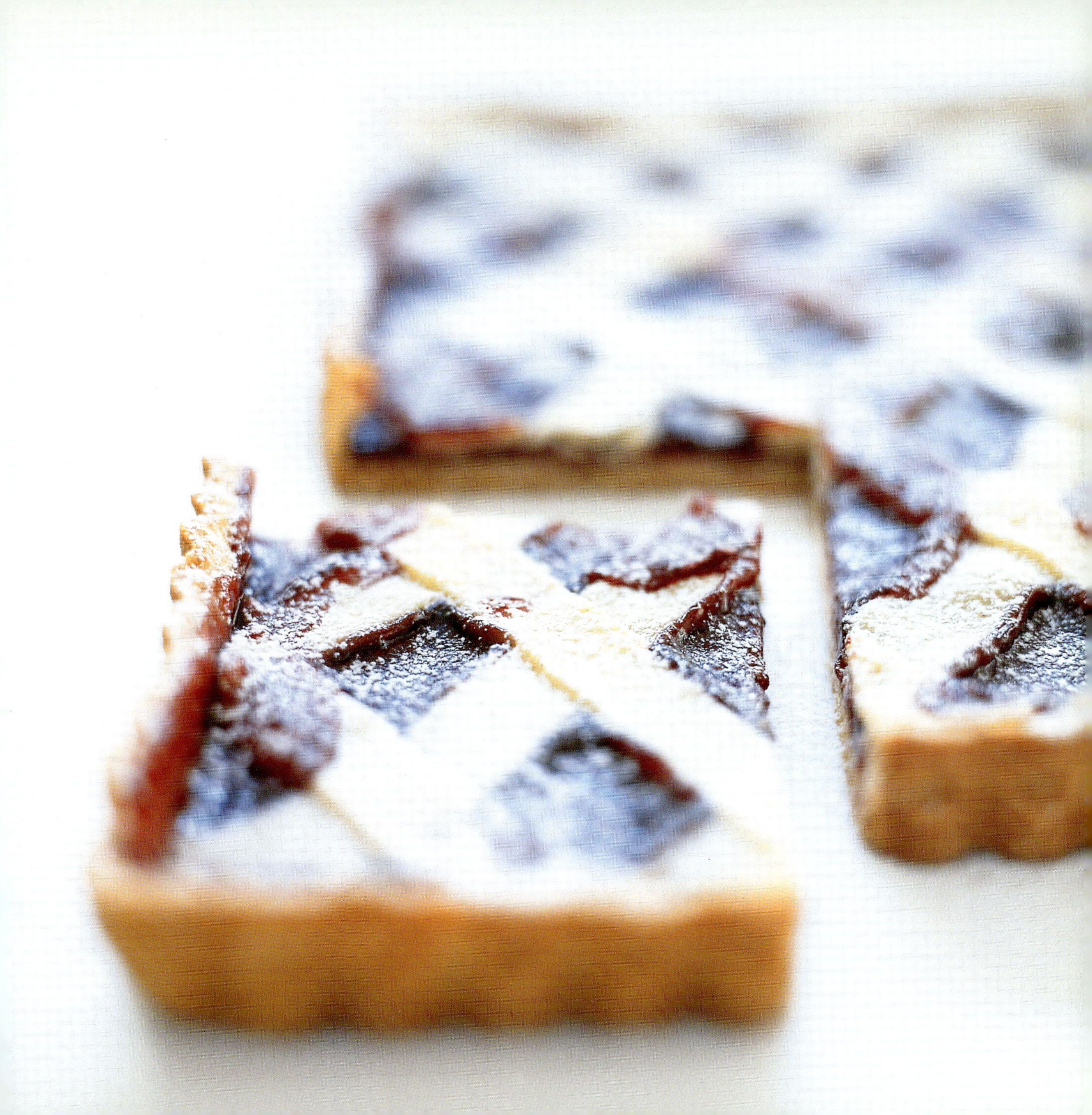

Lemon tart

For the sweet pie crust
2 cups flour
5½ tablespoons superfine sugar
pinch of salt
4 oz unsalted butter
1 egg
1 teaspoon sour cream

For the filling
⅔ cup sour cream
4 eggs
1¼ cups confectioners' sugar
1 cup lemon juice
grated zest of 1 lemon

To make the crust: put the flour, sugar, and salt into a large bowl. Add the butter and with a knife cut it into the flour until evenly distributed, then use your fingertips to rub the fat lightly into the flour until the mixture resembles coarse crumbs. Whisk together the egg and sour cream and add gradually to the crumb mixture (you may not need all of it). Using a spatula or a knife, work the mixture together, then use your fingers until you have a smooth dough. Shape into a ball, put into a plastic bag and refrigerate for 1 hour before using

Preheat the oven to 375°F. Lightly butter a removable bottom tart pan, or small individual pans. Roll out the dough and use to line the pan. Prick the base with a fork. To bake blind: cover the crust with a round of baking parchment and weight with dry beans or pie weights. Bake for 10 minutes. Remove from the oven and take out the weights. Set aside.

Lower the oven to 275°F.

To make the filling: warm the sour cream in a pan over low heat. In a bowl, whisk together the eggs, sugar, and lemon juice. Stir in the warm sour cream and the grated zest. Pour the filling into the prebaked tart shell.

Bake until the filling is just set, about 35 minutes. Let cool before unmoulding. Refrigerate for several hours before serving.

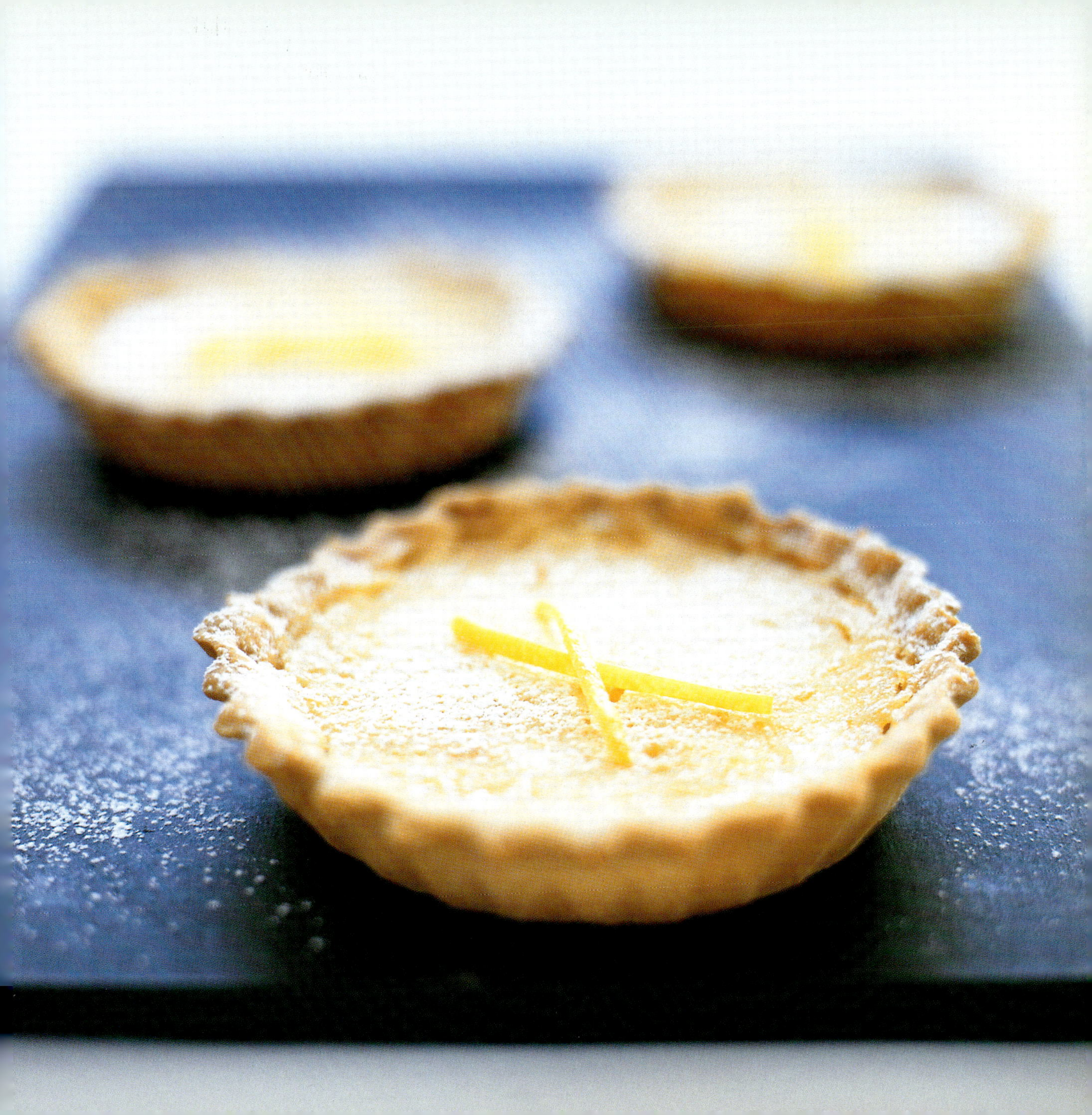

Chestnut tart

For the sweet pie crust
2 cups all-purpose flour
5½ tablespoons superfine sugar
pinch of salt
4 oz unsalted butter
1 egg
1 teaspoon sour cream

For the filling
2 eggs
⅔ cup sour cream
7 oz unsweetened chestnut purée (see note below)
4 tablespoons honey
½ cup slivered almonds, plus a few for decoration

To make the crust: put the flour, sugar, and salt into a large bowl. Add the butter and with a knife cut it into the flour until evenly distributed, then use your fingertips to rub the fat lightly into the flour until the mixture resembles coarse crumbs. Whisk together the egg and sour cream and add gradually to the crumb mixture (you may not need all of it). Using a spatula or a knife, work the mixture together, then use your fingers until you have a smooth dough. Shape into a ball, put into a plastic bag and refrigerate for 1 hour before using

Preheat the oven to 375°F. Lightly butter a removable bottom tart pan. Roll out the dough and use to line the pan. Prick the base with a fork. To bake blind: cover the crust with a round of baking parchment and weight with dry beans or pie weights. Bake for 20 minutes. Remove from the oven and take out the weights. Set aside.

To make the filling: put the eggs, sour cream, chestnut purée, honey, and the almonds in a bowl and stir well to blend. Pour into the prebaked tart shell.

Bake for 20 minutes. Sprinkle with the remaining slivered almonds and let cool before serving.

Note: If unsweetened chestnut purée is unavailable, use canned or vacuum-packed whole peeled chestnuts and purée in a food processor.

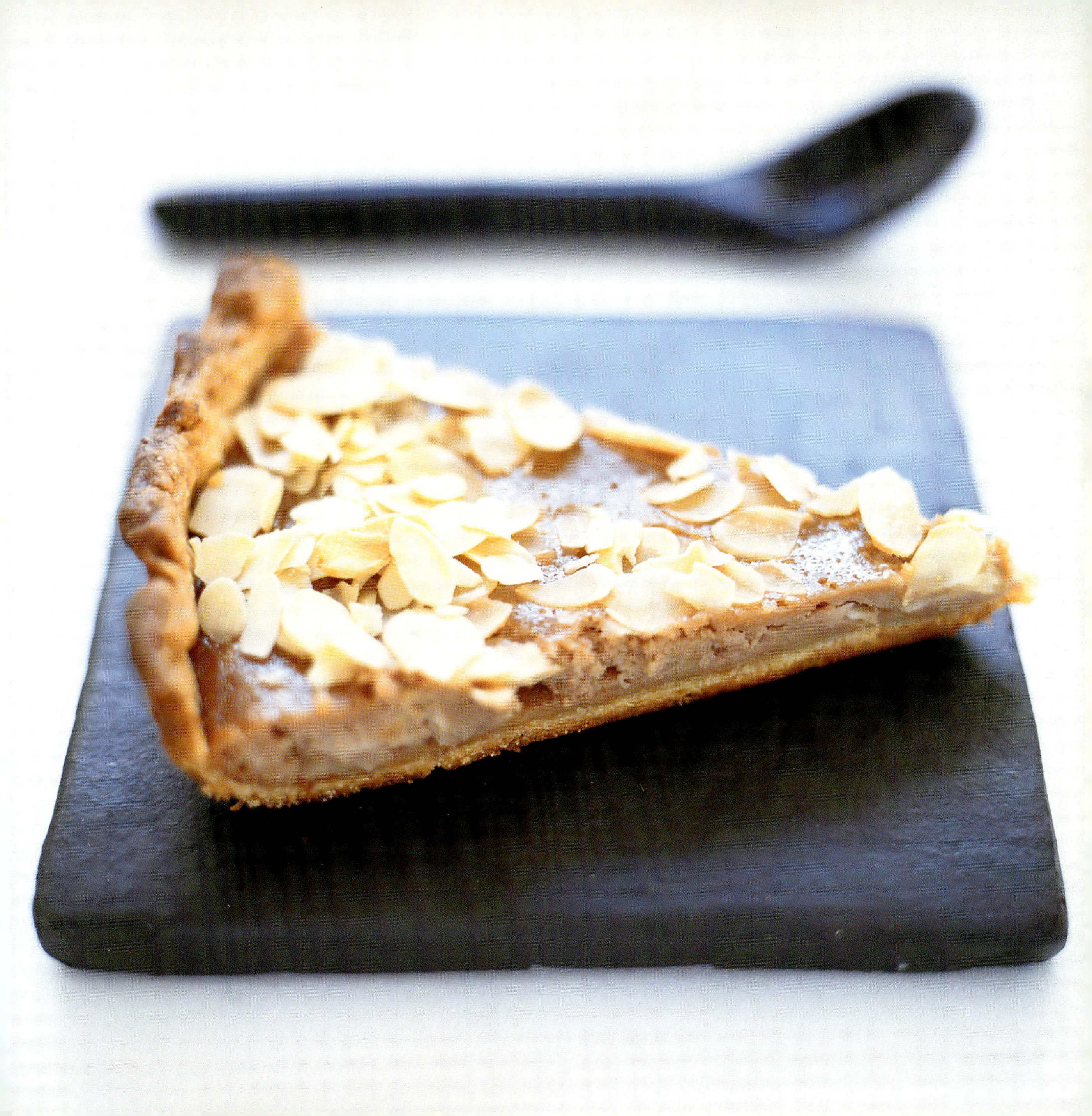

Carrot and walnut cake

2 eggs
½ cup superfine sugar
1½ cups all-purpose flour
4 oz unsalted butter, melted
3 teaspoons baking powder
pinch of bicarbonate of soda
1¼ cups grated carrots
½ cup chopped walnuts
½ teaspoon ground cinnamon

Preheat the oven to 350°F. Grease a loaf pan and dust lightly with flour.

In a bowl, whisk together the eggs and sugar until thick and frothy. Gradually incorporate the flour and melted butter. With a spatula, fold in the baking powder, bicarbonate of soda, carrots, walnuts, and cinnamon. Fold just until well blended.

Pour the batter into the prepared pan and bake for about 50 minutes, until the tip of a knife inserted in the center of the loaf comes out clean. Let cool in the pan before unmoulding.

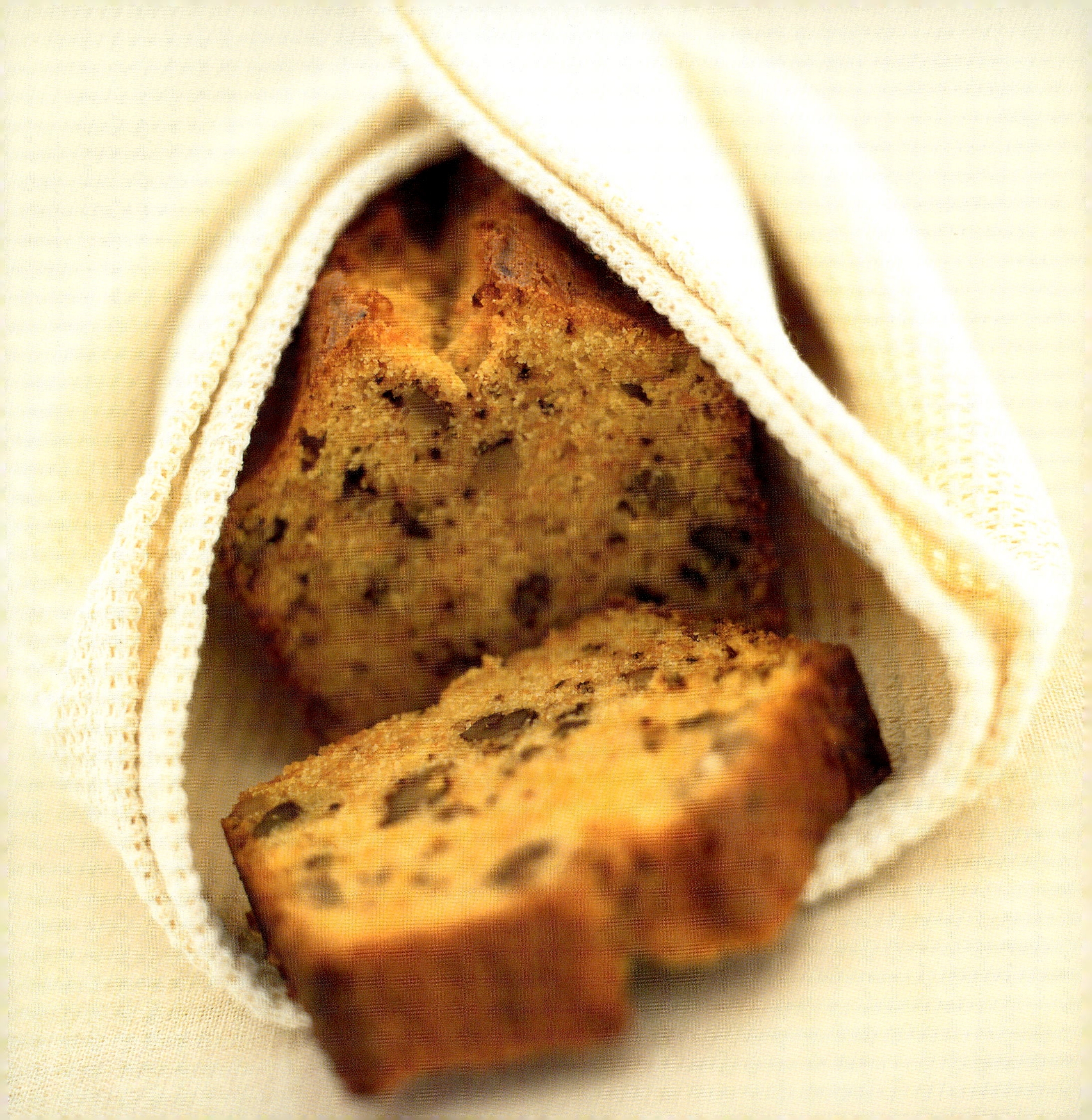

Lemon poppyseed loaf

2 unwaxed lemons
3 eggs
1 scant cup superfine sugar
1½ cups all-purpose flour
5 oz unsalted butter, melted
3 teaspoons baking powder
pinch of bicarbonate of soda
1 tablespoon poppy seeds

Preheat the oven to 350°F. Grease a loaf pan and dust lightly with flour.

Wash the lemons. Grate the zest of 1 lemon and squeeze the juice from both. In a large bowl, whisk together the eggs and sugar until thick and frothy. Gradually incorporate the flour and melted butter. With a spatula, fold in the baking powder, bicarbonate of soda, lemon juice and zest, and poppy seeds. Fold just until well blended.

Pour the batter into the prepared pan and bake for about 50 minutes, until the tip of a knife inserted in the center of the loaf comes out clean. Let cool in the pan before unmoulding.

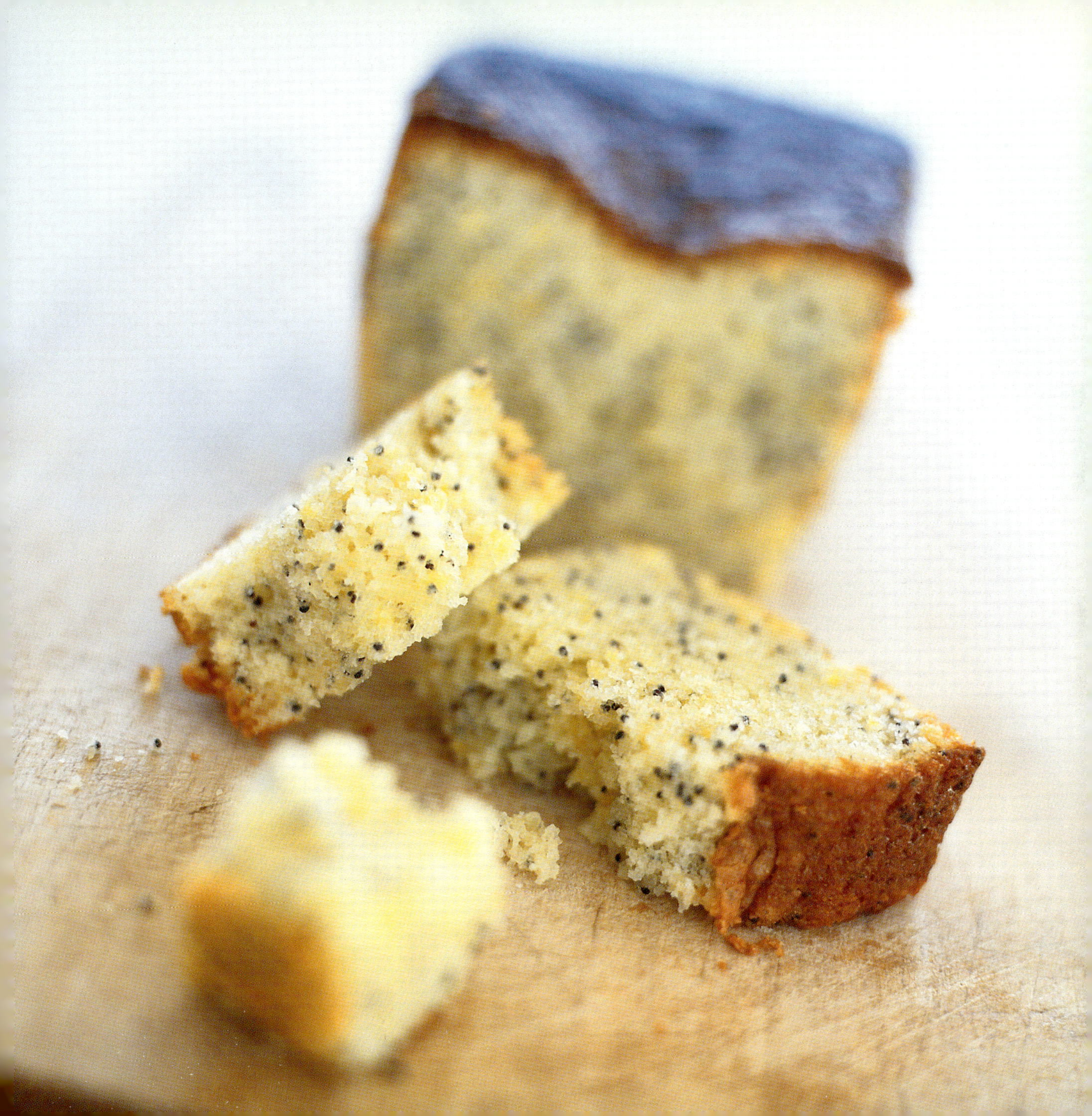

sweet loaves

Candied fruit and nut loaf

½ cup raisins
5 egg whites
¾ cup superfine sugar
2 tablespoons unsalted butter, melted
¾ cup all-purpose flour
½ cup walnut pieces
½ cup finely chopped candied fruit
pinch of salt

Soak the raisins in water or rum. Preheat the oven to 350°F. Grease a loaf pan and dust lightly with flour.

In a bowl, beat the egg whites until firm. Gradually beat in the sugar until stiff and glossy.

With a spatula, fold in the butter, flour, walnuts, drained raisins, and candied fruit. Mix gently to combine.

Pour the batter into the prepared pan and bake for about 50 minutes, until the tip of a knife inserted in the center of the loaf comes out clean. Let cool in the pan before unmoulding.

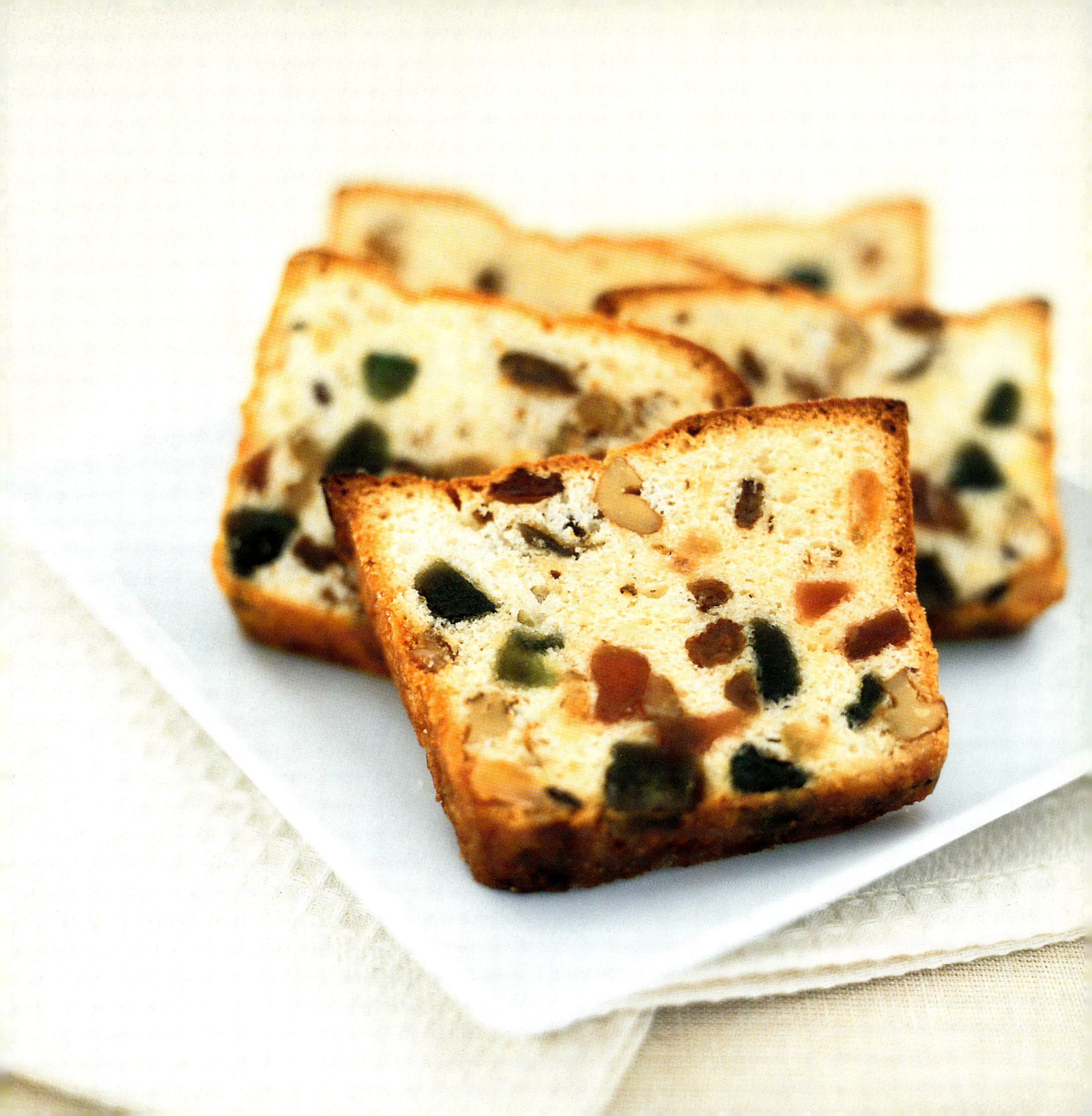

sweet loaves

Apple, raisin and walnut cake

1 tablespoon raisins
3 eggs
1 scant cut superfine sugar
1½ cups all-purpose flour
5 oz unsalted butter, melted
3 teaspoons baking powder
pinch of bicarbonate of soda
1½ cups grated apples
½ cup walnut pieces
½ teaspoon ground cinnamon

Soak the raisins in water for 30 minutes. Preheat the oven to 350°F. Grease a loaf pan and dust lightly with flour.

In a large bowl, whisk together the eggs and sugar until thick and frothy. Gradually incorporate the flour and melted butter. With a spatula, fold in the baking powder, bicarbonate of soda, drained raisins, apples, walnuts, and cinnamon. Fold just until well blended.

Pour the batter into the prepared pan and bake for about 50 minutes, until the tip of a knife inserted in the center of the loaf comes out clean. Let cool in the pan before unmoulding.

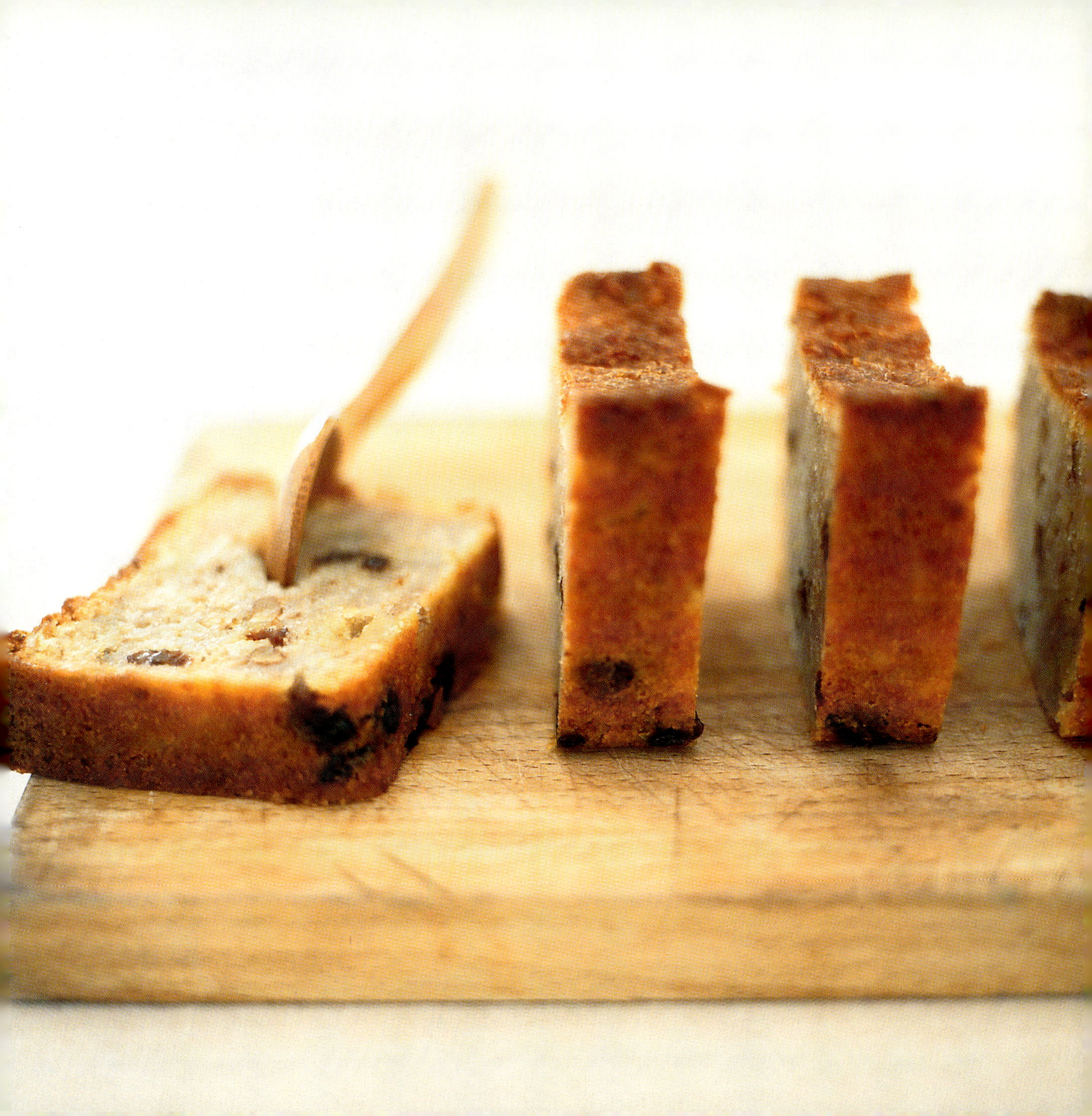

Marble cake with almonds

2 tablespoons milk
2 tablespoons unsweetened cocoa powder
3 eggs
1½ cups confectioners' sugar
1½ cups all-purpose flour
5 oz unsalted butter, melted
3 teaspoons baking powder
3 oz bittersweet chocolate (not unsweetened) or dark European chocolate (at least 70% solids), grated
½ cup slivered almonds

Preheat the oven to 350°F. Grease a loaf pan and dust lightly with flour.

Mix together the milk and cocoa powder in a small bowl. Set aside.

In a large bowl, whisk together the eggs and sugar until thick and frothy. Add the baking powder to the flour and gradually incorporate into the eggs and sugar. Add the melted butter. Divide the batter equally between two bowls. In the first bowl, gently fold in the milk and cocoa powder and the grated chocolate. In the second bowl, fold in the almonds.

Pour half the chocolate batter into the prepared pan, top with half the almond batter. Then add the remaining half of the chocolate batter and finish with the rest of the almond batter. Using a knife swirl gently through all the layers just enough to marble. Bake for about 50 minutes, until the tip of a knife inserted in the center of the loaf comes out clean. Let cool in the pan before unmoulding.

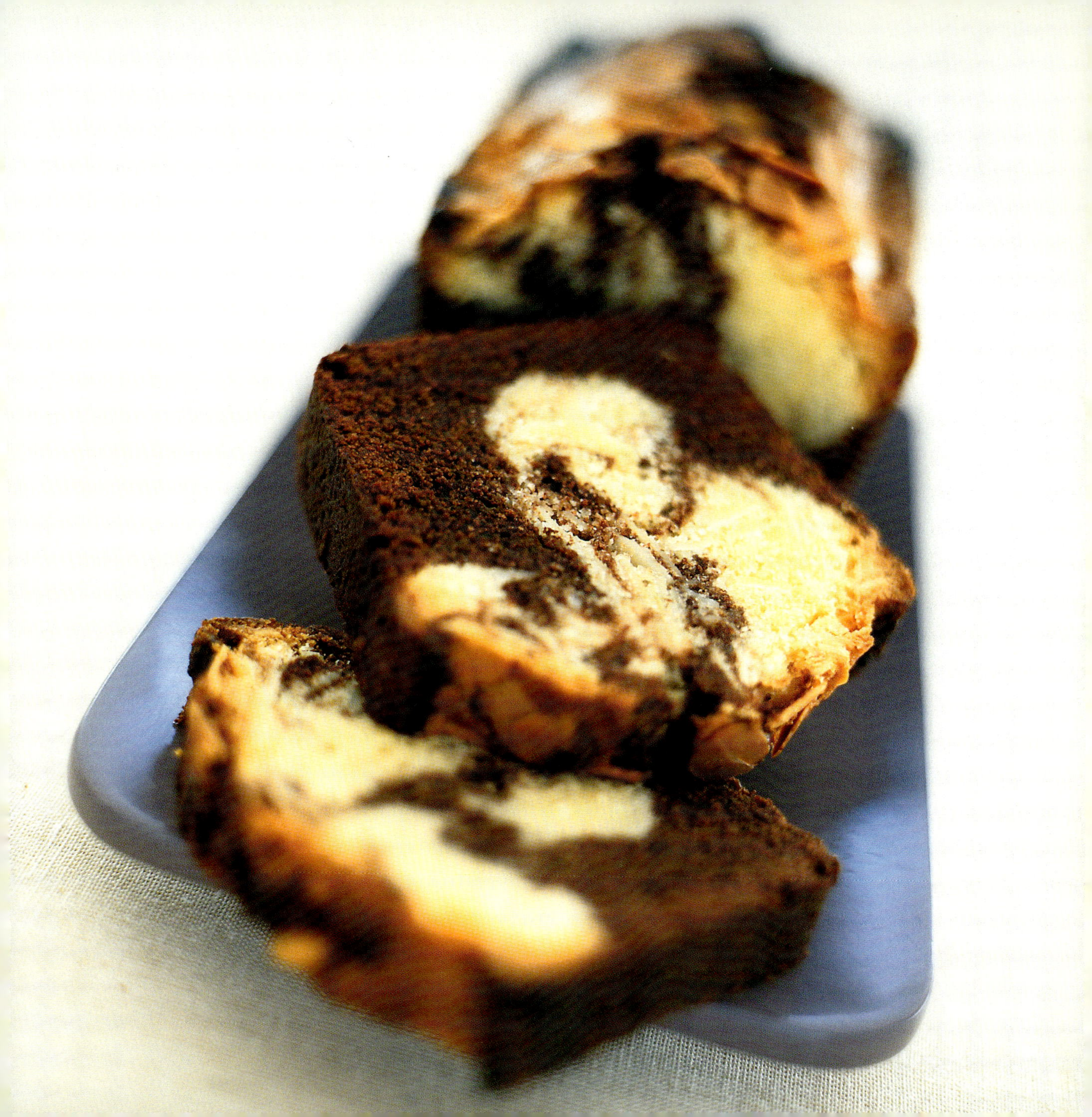

sweet loaves

Mixed berry loaf

3 eggs
$\frac{1}{2}$ cup superfine sugar
$\frac{7}{8}$ cup all-purpose flour
$\frac{7}{8}$ cup whole-wheat flour
3 oz unsalted butter, melted
3 teaspoons baking powder
pinch of bicarbonate of soda
$\frac{1}{2}$ cup plain yogurt
$1\frac{3}{4}$ cups mixed berries (blueberries, raspberries, blackberries, redcurrants, etc.)

Preheat the oven to 350°F. Grease a loaf pan and dust lightly with flour.

In a large bowl, whisk together the eggs and sugar until thick and frothy. Gradually incorporate both the flours and melted butter. With a spatula, fold in the baking powder, bicarbonate of soda, yogurt, and berries. Fold just until well blended.

Pour the batter into the prepared pan and bake for about 50 minutes, until the tip of a knife inserted in the center of the loaf comes out clean. Let cool in the pan before unmoulding.

glossary

bicarbonate of soda This fine white powder is an indispensable raising agent ingredient when baking sweet cakes. Just a pinch will lighten the batter and makes it easier to digest. It is readily available in large supermarkets and sometimes at the pharmacy (be sure to indicate that it is for culinary use). Always use the quantities indicated in the recipe.

candied fruit Fruit that has been cooked in syrup then coated with sugar. When baking with candied fruit, be sure to dust it with flour before adding to the mixture so that the pieces do not sink to the bottom.

capers in salt These are the smallest and most sought after form of capers, and are usually found in specialist delicatessens. Before using, they should be rinsed under running water and then left to drain in a colander. Alternatively, they can be soaked in cold water for 15 minutes.

dusting a cake pan To make sure that you cake won't stick to the sides and bottom of the pan, grease it well with butter, then sprinkle in some flour and tilt the pan to spread evenly. Tap the pan firmly and tip out any excess flour.

feta Greek cheese made from goat or sheep's milk, with a hard and crumbly texture. It is sold in slices, or cubed in jars with a marinade of olive oil and herbs.

mozzarella Fresh, stringy cheese, in the form of a ball, that is made from the curdled milk of cows or buffalo. Mozzarella is readily available in most large supermarkets and Italian delicatessens.

parmesan Very hard cheese, made from cows' milk. Aging depends on the type, but the famous Italian variety, Parmigiano-Reggiano, is aged for at least 2 years before it can be sold. It is best to buy whole chunks of Parmesan to grate as needed; the ready-grated cheese has less flavor and does not keep well as it dries out quickly.

peeled tomatoes Tomatoes that have the skins removed before they are canned, sometimes also flavored with basil and other herbs. These are widely available in a variety of forms including whole, chopped, crushed, and stewed.

pesto This sauce, also known as pistou, is made from a purée of basil, garlic, pine nuts, Parmesan, olive oil, and coarse salt (see page 4).

pine nuts These are the seeds from the cone of several varieties of pine trees. Available in most large supermarkets, in the dried fruit and nut section.

pink peppercorns These are not true peppercorns but the dried berry of a South American rose plant. They are found in large supermarkets or specialty food stores, either dried or packed in vinegar. Adding these pink peppercorns to a dish gives it an attractive appearance as well as pleasant flavor.

poppyseeds These come from a plant that is cultivated especially for its seeds, used mainly in bread, cakes, and pastries. Poppyseeds are available in large supermarkets and health food stores.

pumpkin Cut into quarters, remove the seeds and peel. Cooks very quickly.

ricotta This cheese is made from the whey left over after making other cows' milk cheeses. The name derives from the Italian for "re-cooking". Its texture and flavor make it a useful ingredient for both sweet and savory dishes. Ricotta can be found in most supermarkets, usually in tubs.

sun-dried tomatoes Known as pomodori secchi in Italy, these are traditionally dried in the sun, then preserved in oil. To make them at home, dry out the tomatoes in a low oven for about 3 hours. Transfer to a sterilized jar and marinate with garlic, olive oil, salt, and pepper for 2–3 weeks (see page 4). These are also available in most large supermarkets and Italian delicatessens.

whipping cream This cream contains not less than 35% butterfat, which enables it to be whipped, unlike single cream that has 18% and cannot be whipped.

wholegrain mustard Dijon-style mustard with the addition of whole mustard seeds.

zest Very thin strips of lemon or other citrus rind, used to flavor sweet and savory dishes, and some drinks.

Shopping: Yves Deshoulières/
Blanc d'Ivoire

© Marabout 2001
text © Ilona C.
photographs © Akiko Ida

© Hachette 2001
This edition © 2003 Hachette Illustrated UK, Octopus Publishing Group,
2–4 Heron Quays, London E14 4JP
English translation by JMS Books LLP
(email: moseleystrachan@blueyonder.co.uk)
Translation © Octopus Publishing Group

All rights reserved. No part of this publication may be reproduced in material form (including photocopying or storing it in any medium by electronic means and whether or not transiently or incidentally to some other use of this publication) without the written permission of the copyright owner, except in accordance with the provisions of the Copyright, Designs and Patents Act 1988 or under the terms of a licence issued by the Copyright Licensing Agency,
90 Tottenham Court Road, London W1P 9HE.

A CIP catalogue for this book is available from the British Library

ISBN: 1 84430 045 5

Printed by Tien Wah, Singapore